CANAPÉS

AND

Frivolities

CANAPÉS

AND

Frivolities

ANTON EDELMANN

JANE SUTHERING

RECIPES FROM THE SAVOY · LONDON

Photographs by Michael Boys

PAVILION

ACKNOWLEDGEMENTS

We would like to thank:

The Directors and Management of The Savoy,
especially Mr Giles Shepard and Mr Herbert Striessnig for their help
and generosity during the writing of this book.

Peter Dorelli, Head Barman at The Savoy, who has kindly
created a new cocktail for each chapter of the book.

The Chefs in The Savoy kitchens especially Gordon Dochard,
Julian Jenkins, Andrew Huxley and Anthony Robinson.

Meg Jansz for her help in testing the recipes for domestic cooking.

First published in Great Britain in 1991 by
PAVILION BOOKS LIMITED
196 Shaftesbury Avenue, London WC2H 8JL

Text copyright © Anton Edelmann and Jane Suthering 1991
Photographs copyright © Michael Boys 1991

Designed by Janet James

Cocktail illustrations by Katherine Greenwood

A CIP catalogue record for this book is
available from the British Library

ISBN 1 85145 587 6

10 9 8 7 6 5 4 3 2 1
Printed and bound in Germany
by Mohndruck

All tiles photographed courtesy of
Fired Earth Tiles Plc, Oxford.

CONTENTS

INTRODUCTION

Some people eat to live. Others, the kind of people I know, eat and cook when awake and dream of food when they sleep. Is it an obsession, is it plain greed? I don't believe it really matters; all that really counts is the enjoyment of eating and a genuine love for cooking.

The longer you study and practise this art, the more you realise the depths of the subject. It does not matter how many years you have been cooking, you may have only just touched the surface, but there is reward even in anticipation of the great joys of discovery.

Food should be respected and taken seriously, if only because it is such an important factor in our daily lives. It is not, however, a religion and eating should never become a pretentious and affected pastime. But the rituals of preparation and consumption should be followed and adhered to because, to my mind, these form the fine dividing line between the gourmand and gourmet.

I have my own theory about the history of food. It has always played a very important part in the development of mankind. As far back as Ancient Egyptian times, there is reference to the seven 'fat' years and seven 'lean' years. I wonder what the Bible was trying to tell us? Surely the lesson was not to be selfish and narrow-minded, but charitable towards others. And then again, when Jesus blessed the bread and the fish on the hill, was he not really telling us to share our food with others and enjoy it in their company? He even remembered the wine, which of course stimulates the appetite, as well as an atmosphere of companionship and conviviality.

I have been endlessly fascinated by the discovery and the import of certain foods. Marco Polo, for instance, brought pasta back to Italy from his travels in China, eventually influencing the whole of world food culture. The Italian Medicis, when they married into the French aristocracy, brought fine cuisine to France and established it in that society as an art form. The arrival of Christopher Columbus in the New World in 1498 brought us many new ingredients now essential to twentieth-century cooking – the humble yet delicious potato springs to mind. Cocoa, cultivated by the Mayo Indians in New Mexico and believed to be a strong aphrodisiac, was brought back by the Spanish conquerors all too willingly!

English high society and European aristocracy then brought us the first superstar chef, Antoine Carême, who cooked for kings, kaisers and tsars, and was given the title 'Emperor of all Chefs'. He also had the foresight to record all of his work in the form of a book, becoming one of the founders of the tradition of cookery writing.

Around the turn of the century, the building of great elegant hotels, such as The Savoy in 1889, caused another style of eating to evolve. The rich, titled and regal, instead of eating only at home, went out to dine in the luxurious restaurants of these hotels, a trend started by César Ritz. This, in turn, brought a new kind of chef, one who was required to be creative, imaginative and technically highly skilled. Auguste Escoffier at The Savoy was the first of this new breed of chefs, and many of his dishes became classics, such as the Peach Melba he created for the Australian operatic soprano Nellie Melba, and Frogs Legs Aurore for the Prince of Wales. He also revolutionised the layout and work flow of the hotel kitchens, putting the chefs in white uniform and establishing a hierarchy of tall white hats now identified with chefs all over the world. The man was a genius.

Since those days, eating and cooking have developed at an ever-increasing pace. The world has become a smaller place with the advance of modern transport, and there is very little that is not available to us all the year round – a sad fact, perhaps, if you consider that lost anticipation of certain fruits, vegetables, fish and meats in season.

Far-off cultures and civilisations have made their impact – ethnic food is now firmly part of our everyday eating habits. However, there is a strong nostalgic streak in the recent return to traditional home-cooking, which is, I believe, always the backbone of a civilised cuisine. Food incites a host of different emotions and responses, but most often it comforts us and gives us strength and security. We also celebrate special occasions, personal, business or religious, with food. It is nourishment, both physical and psychological, if eaten with awareness and in the right quantities. It can bring discomfort and much worse if abused!

But above all, as arguably the greatest pleasure in life, food should be interesting and varied, and never closed to new flavours and textures. Good cooks take risks in exploring and experimenting; they create the right atmosphere in which to enjoy good food and good company – a form of heaven for cook, Maître Chef and guest alike.

The paths to this heaven are many, but one of the most innovative and contemporary is with canapés and frivolities: small pieces of food, attractive in their colours and shapes, contrasting in their textures and flavours. Whether highly spiced, or subtly herbed, whether wildly exotic in flavour or gutsily familiar, they can be both a sensual and aesthetic joy. Their ingredients can vary enormously, from simple garlic to expensive caviar, from fromage frais to rich goose liver pâté, and their preparations vary from the extremely simple – left almost in their natural state – to the very sophisticated and intricate. In their methods of cooking, some take only a matter of minutes, whilst others are quite labour-intensive and time-consuming. In their presentations, they range from the traditional and elegant to the highly designed and utterly breathtaking.

The origin of this food must lie in the earliest of civilisations, at the moment when eating became social rather than simply life sustaining.

The whole basis of *Canapés and Frivolities* is a light-hearted approach to cooking and entertaining. This book offers a vast selection of whatever your heart desires or the occasion demands. Ideas for specific parties can be found on pages 140-1, but always bear the following points in mind.

THE OCCASION

This will probably be the biggest factor in deciding what you offer your guests. Is it a business meeting or the conclusion of a deal and therefore fairly formal? This obviously requires a different approach from that of inviting a few friends around for a drink and a little something to eat.

TIME OF DAY AND DURATION

If it is a little get-together before lunch you will not require enormous quantities of food. However, if it is a two or three hour affair at noon or early evening it needs to be quite extensive – there's nothing worse than a lack of food at a drinks party and you certainly don't want your guests to fall over after their second or third glass!

SEASON AND LOCATION

These two points always need to be given a lot of consideration. There is no point in serving expensive asparagus or raspberries in January when something like salmon pasties would be just the right thing from a seasonal point of view as well as more substantial as a winter canapé.

The time of year will also determine the location of the party – whether you plan to have it in the garden during the summer or in front of an open fire in autumn. The location will also influence the style of food, the presentation and the service or indeed the whole theme of the party.

AGE GROUP AND WHAT TO DRINK

This is a very important point which can make a huge impact. Not all of us can choose to serve Champagne all the time. A cold punch in the summer prepared with a dry white or sparkling wine, or a mulled wine in the winter to start with (see Magic Punch page 104), or even a trendy cocktail for young people can be a lot of fun.

Many people nowadays prefer a straight drink to mixers so that they can judge their alcohol intake and indeed may choose to drink little or no alcohol at all. There is quite a good selection of low-alcohol wines available now, so do have a good look around.

PLANNING THE MENU

Having taken all the previous points into consideration, there is now the fun of choosing the individual canapés – which can bring its own particular problems. So here are some more guidelines:

a) How much time and help have I got; how much can I do the day before; what needs to be done at the last moment?
b) How much time do I want to spend in the kitchen at the last moment. The answer to that must be as little as possible as you want to spend as much time as you can with your guests.
c) The timing of when to serve what.

It is always advisable to start a small party with just cold canapés as you don't want to offer hot canapés slightly congealed to late arrivals. It also means you can be well organised in advance.

It is also important to keep some cold canapés back for serving later, when the party is thinning out. The sweet side of the affair should be happening about half way through the party so that people who wish to leave early still get the benefit of the whole menu, as well as being a good indication to other guests that they might start to think about leaving!

THE MENU PICTURE

The idea is to offer an interesting variation and a nice cross-section of all kinds of canapés and frivolities. Individually they must look and taste excellent, but their combination is equally important. In planning the menu you should consider:-

Colour variation in the final display

Texture of component ingredients

Repetition of ingredients

Nutritional value plus all the modern considerations of health and calories

Good balance of hot and cold, savoury and sweet

Cooking and preparation methods

Choice of serving dishes and how they are presented: will they be passed around or will they be dotted strategically around the room?

PLANNING THE PREPARATION

Try to do as much as possible one or two days ahead. Prepare hot canapés to the stage where they just have to be cooked – be it frying, grilling or baking. One should work as precisely as possible and this can only be done if you have sufficient time.

NOTE TO AMERICAN COOKS

The ingredients have been given wherever practical in metric, imperial and volume form; cup equivalents have not been used for foods usually sold by weight, for example cheese. It is important to follow only one set of measures as these are not interchangeable.

In recipes where a specific quantity of pastry is given, this refers to the overall weight of the prepared pastry (dough).

If using a fan-assisted oven, follow the manufacturer's instructions regarding temperatures.

CRAB CHEQUERBOARD

QUICK

A N D

Simple

There's a well-known saying which goes something like 'What is right in front of your eyes, you very seldom see', and so this chapter is all about improvisation and imagination, although, of course, a little planning always helps. If unexpected visitors turn up on your doorstep and a look in the larder doesn't reveal interesting or vast quantities of food, do not despair.

A piece of fried chicken breast on hot buttered toast flavoured with tomato ketchup and horseradish will delight guests and leave them amazed at your resourcefulness at such short notice. This will undoubtedly add to an atmosphere of relaxation and cheerfulness, in which no one could possibly feel unwelcome.

Small grissini sticks, snippets of Parma ham (prosciutto) and plums, salami with cherry tomatoes or even something as simple and traditional as the French croque monsieur cut in neat pieces can be put together very quickly and nicely presented. What could be more complimentary than to be known as an inventive and cheerful party maker?

DECEPTION

A long drink with quite a kick! Created
by Peter Dorelli, Head Barman at
The Savoy.

⅔ vodka
⅓ midori (melon-flavoured liqueur)

Top up with lemonade and decorate with
a slice of orange and a cherry.

CRAB CHEQUERBOARD

MAKES ABOUT 30

100g/4oz white crab meat
2 tablespoons mayonnaise (see page 137)
lemon juice
cayenne
100g/4oz brown crab meat
1 teaspoon freshly chopped mint
40g/1½oz/3 tablespoons unsalted butter,
softened
2 teaspoons English (dry) made mustard
8 slices of brown bread from a large sliced loaf
2 hard-boiled eggs
1 tablespoon freshly chopped parsley
salt and freshly milled pepper

Mix the white crab meat with half the mayonnaise and then season to taste with lemon juice, cayenne and salt. Mix the brown crab meat with the remaining mayonnaise and the mint. Season to taste.

Mix the butter and mustard together and spread on the slices of bread. Cut off the crusts.

Spread the white crab meat on four slices of the bread. Spread the brown crab meat on the remaining slices. Then cut in quarters.

Separate the egg whites and yolks and pass each through a fine sieve. Sprinkle the egg white on the white crab meat pieces and sprinkle with chopped parsley. Sprinkle the egg yolk on the brown crab meat pieces.

Arrange all the pieces chequerboard-fashion on a serving plate or board.

PHOTOGRAPH ON PAGE 10

PRAWN (SHRIMP) PROFITEROLES

Britain's consistently best loved starter – prawn cocktail – served in a nest.

MAKES ABOUT 40

For the choux paste:
250ml/8fl oz/1 cup milk
90g/3½oz/7 tablespoons unsalted butter
150g/5oz/1¼ cups plain (all-purpose)
flour, sifted
¾ teaspoon salt
4 eggs, beaten
beaten egg to glaze
finely chopped pistachio nuts to sprinkle

For the filling:
150g/5oz/¾ cup crisp lettuce leaves,
very finely shredded
120ml/4fl oz/½ cup cocktail sauce (see
page 136)
450g/1lb peeled prawns (shrimp),
thoroughly drained

Place the milk and butter in a saucepan and heat until the butter is melted. Bring to the boil, then reduce the heat. Add the flour and salt and stir well until the mixture forms a smooth paste. Cook, stirring constantly, for a further minute.

Cool the mixture slightly, then beat in the egg a little at a time.

Using a piping bag fitted with a 1cm/⅜ inch plain nozzle (tube), pipe about 40 mounds of choux paste on to lightly buttered baking trays. Brush with beaten egg and press lightly with the prongs of a fork. Sprinkle with pistachio nuts.

Bake in a preheated oven at 220°C/425°F/gas mark 7 for about 20 minutes until crisp and golden. Transfer to a wire tray. Split each profiterole to allow the steam to escape.

When cold, place a small amount of lettuce in each profiterole, top with about ½ teaspoon cocktail sauce and a few prawns (shrimp). Replace each lid.

GRISSINI FRANCESCA

Now a lunchtime favourite of two-year-old Francesca Edelmann, these grissini are delicious with smoked salmon, but other smoked fish such as tuna or halibut, or even Parma Ham, may be used.

MAKES 20

10 grissini sticks
unsalted butter for spreading
175g/6oz smoked salmon, thinly sliced

Break the grissini sticks in half and spread them lightly with butter, leaving 1.5cm/2 inches unbuttered at the broken end of each one.

Cut the smoked salmon in 20 strips about 1.5cm/½ inch wide and wrap a strip in a spiral around the buttered portion of each grissini.

RIVIERA TARTLETS

These tartlets flavoured with truffle oil are best made with organically grown tomatoes, which have what is termed in wine tasting 'a big nose'.

Truffle oil is available commercially or can be made by marinating a whole truffle in a bottle of extra virgin olive oil.

MAKES ABOUT 30

350g/12oz puff pastry
3 tablespoons julienne of fresh basil leaves
50g/2oz/scant ½ cup Parmesan cheese, grated
6 organic or plum tomatoes, blanched and peeled
1 tablespoon truffle oil
5 tablespoons sunflower oil
½ teaspoon balsamic or sherry vinegar
salt and freshly milled pepper

On a lightly floured surface, roll out the puff pastry about 3mm/⅛ inch thick and stamp out about 30 5-6.5cm/2-2½ inch rounds, using the trimmings as necessary. Leave to rest in a cool place for at least 20 minutes. Prick with a fork and bake in a preheated oven at 200°C/400°F/gas mark 6 for about 10 minutes until golden.

Flatten the pastry rounds, then sprinkle with the basil julienne and half the Parmesan cheese. Cut the tomatoes in slices and place one on each pastry base. Season with salt and pepper.

Combine the oils and vinegar and brush a little over the tomatoes. Sprinkle the remaining Parmesan cheese on top and return to the oven for about 5 minutes. Serve at once.

PAILLETTES

Paillettes are altogether undervalued. They should always be made with Parmesan cheese but can be flavoured with all sorts of herbs, seeds and spices and cut into all kinds of shapes – thick, thin, long or large – served individually or in a pyramid. They can be prepared in advance and baked at the last moment.

MAKES ABOUT 50

250g/9oz puff pastry
beaten egg to glaze
50g/2oz/scant ½ cup Parmesan cheese, grated
1½ teaspoons freshly chopped rosemary
1½ teaspoons freshly chopped sage
1 teaspoon paprika
2 teaspoons caraway seeds

On a lightly floured surface, roll out the pastry about 3mm/⅛ inch thick. Cut in three equal portions. Brush with beaten egg and sprinkle each portion with Parmesan cheese, then sprinkle one portion with the herbs, and another with paprika and caraway seeds.

Fold the pastry over in half again and roll each piece out 3mm/⅛ inch thick. Cut the pastry in strips about 15cm/6 inches long and 5mm/¼ inch wide. Roll each strip with your hands, working in opposite directions to achieve a twisted effect. Leave to rest for at least 20 minutes in a cool place.

Bake on lightly greased baking trays in a preheated oven at 200°C/400°F/gas mark 6 for 10-12 minutes until the pastry is crisp and golden.

PESTO MOONS

Pine kernels, basil, olives and anchovy form the spine of the great Mediterranean cuisines. Serve with a good Italian country wine.

MAKES 30

175g/6oz puff pastry
beaten egg to glaze
3 plum tomatoes, cut in 30 half slices – use red or yellow
8 stoned (pitted) black olives, quartered
8 anchovy fillets, quartered
8 teaspoons pesto (see page 135)
75g/3oz Mozzarella cheese, cut in 60 diamond shapes

Roll out the pastry on a lightly floured surface to a 30cm/12 inch square. Brush the pastry with beaten egg.

Arrange four rows of tomato slices 2.5cm/1 inch apart on the pastry. Top each tomato slice with a piece of olive, a piece of anchovy and a little pesto. Starting at the bottom of each row, stamp out three-quarter moon shapes around each tomato slice, using a 6.5cm/2½ inch cutter. Leave to rest in a cool place for at least 20 minutes.

Place on a lightly greased baking tray and bake in a preheated oven at 220°C/425°F/gas mark 7 for about 10 minutes until the pastry is crisp.

Place two diamond shapes of Mozzarella cheese on each one and glaze under a preheated grill (broiler) until just melted. Serve at once.

PUFF PASTRY HEARTS AND DISCS
PAILLETTES
PESTO MOONS

DIP AND DIVE

Make one or more of the dips given on page 17 and serve with crisp biscuits (crackers) or puff pastry shapes. Serve in small quantities replenishing as required.

PUFF PASTRY HEARTS AND DISCS

These light pastries are delicious with dips. Alternatively, they may be split and filled with a rosette of piped cheese made by combining equal quantities of double cream and sieved blue cheese, such as Roquefort or Stilton, and beating until smooth.

MAKES 40

150g/5oz puff pastry
1 egg yolk, beaten
2 teaspoons poppy or sesame seeds
1 teaspoon paprika

On a lightly floured surface, roll out the pastry about 3mm/⅛ inch thick. Brush with beaten egg and divide in two portions.

Sprinkle one portion with poppy seeds and the other with paprika. Leave to rest in a cool place for at least 20 minutes, then cut out 20 'poppy' hearts and 20 'paprika' discs. Arrange on buttered baking trays and leave to rest for 2 hours.

Bake in a preheated oven at 220-230°C/425-450°F/gas mark 7-8 for about 10 minutes until crisp.

PHOTOGRAPH ON PAGE 15

SANDWICHED CHEESE SABLÉS

Cheddar cheese and mustard combine with poppy seeds to make these wonderful biscuits. Garnish with miniature grapes when available.

MAKES 40

225g/8oz/scant 2 cups plain (all-purpose) flour
1 teaspoon mustard powder
225g/8oz/1 cup unsalted butter
225g/8oz/2½ cups mature Cheddar cheese, grated
salt and freshly milled pepper
beaten egg to glaze
poppy seeds to sprinkle

For the filling:
100g/4oz/1¼ cups mature Cheddar cheese, grated
100g/4oz/½ cup curd cheese
1 teaspoon Dijon mustard
½ teaspoon paprika
1-2 tablespoons milk

Sift the flour and mustard powder together. Rub in the butter, then add the cheese and season generously. Work the mixture together to form a firm dough.

Roll out on a lightly floured surface and stamp out 80 5cm/2 inch rounds. Place the rounds on baking trays and chill for at least 20 minutes.

Brush half the pastry rounds with beaten egg and sprinkle with poppy seeds. Bake in a preheated oven at 190°C/375°F/gas mark 5 for 12-15 minutes until golden brown. Cool on a wire tray.

Combine the ingredients for the filling and beat well to give a spreading consistency. Sandwich the pastry rounds together with the filling, using the poppy seed-coated ones for the tops.

SESAME CRACKERS

MAKES ABOUT 40

50g/2oz/⅓ cup wholemeal (wholewheat) flour
50g/2oz/5 tablespoons plain (all-purpose) flour
½ teaspoon salt
¾ teaspoon baking powder
1 tablespoon sesame seeds plus extra for sprinkling
15g/½oz/1 tablespoon unsalted butter
2 tablespoons yoghurt
2-3 tablespoons water
beaten egg yolk to glaze

Mix the flours, salt and baking powder together.

Lightly fry the sesame seeds in the butter until golden, then add to the flour mixture. Stir in the yoghurt and sufficient water to mix to a firm dough.

On a lightly floured surface, roll out the dough very thinly and cut in small rounds about 4cm/1½ inch diameter. Place on a buttered baking tray and leave to rest in a cool place for 30 minutes.

Brush with egg glaze and sprinkle lightly with sesame seeds. Bake in a preheated oven at 180°C/350°F/gas mark 4 for 10-15 minutes until golden.

MINT AND CUCUMBER DIP

100g/4oz/³⁄₄ cup cucumber, peeled and
finely diced
175g/6oz/³⁄₄ cup cream cheese
12 mint leaves, chopped
2 teaspoons natural yoghurt
4 teaspoons milk
salt and freshly milled pepper

Combine all the ingredients together and beat well. Season to taste.

WARM CHEESE AND ONION DIP

1 tablespoon vegetable oil
75g/3oz/¹⁄₂ cup onion, finely chopped
300ml/¹⁄₂ pint/1¹⁄₄ cups double (heavy) cream
150g/5oz/1¹⁄₄ cups Red Leicester cheese, grated
1 tablespoon freshly chopped chives
salt and freshly milled pepper

Heat the oil and sweat the onion until translucent. Add the cream and bring to the boil, then reduce by half by fast boiling.

Stir in the cheese in small amounts until melted. Stir in the chives and season to taste. Serve at once.

PRAWN AND GINGER DIP

100g/4oz/¹⁄₂ cup peeled cooked prawns
(shrimp), finely chopped
2 tablespoons freshly chopped coriander
(cilantro) leaves
1 teaspoon freshly grated root ginger
¹⁄₂ quantity cocktail sauce (see page 136)

Mix all the ingredients together until evenly combined.

HORSERADISH DIP

300ml/¹⁄₂pint/1¹⁄₄ cups double (heavy) or
whipping cream
1 tablespoon lemon juice or white wine vinegar
1-2 tablespoons freshly grated horseradish
1 tablespoon freshly chopped chives

Lightly whip the cream until it just holds the trail of the whisk. Stir in the remaining ingredients.

TUNA FISH DIP

3 tablespoons olive oil
2 tablespoons finely chopped shallots
¹⁄₂ small clove of garlic, crushed
1 tablespoon tomato purée (paste)
3 tomatoes, skinned, deseeded and chopped
200g/7oz can of tuna fish, drained
400ml/14fl oz/1³⁄₄ cups chicken or
vegetable stock
120ml/4fl oz/¹⁄₂ cup dry white wine
120ml/4fl oz/¹⁄₂ cup double (heavy) cream
salt and freshly milled pepper

Heat the oil and sweat the shallots until translucent; add the garlic and sweat for a further minute. Add the tomato purée, tomatoes, tuna, stock and white wine and simmer for about 30 minutes until the liquid has been absorbed. Leave to cool.

Purée the tuna mixture in a liquidiser (blender) or food processor and leave until cold.

Whip the cream and fold into the tuna mixture. Season to taste.

GARLIC CREAM DIP

3 heads of garlic
25g/1oz/2 tablespoons unsalted butter
2 tablespoons olive oil
1 large onion, sliced
1 fresh bay leaf
300ml/¹⁄₂ pint/1¹⁄₄ cups double (heavy) cream
salt and freshly milled pepper

Peel all the garlic cloves and cut each one in half. Boil the garlic in three changes of water for 5 minutes each time. Drain.

Heat the butter and oil and cook the garlic, onion and bay leaf over a very gentle heat for about 20 minutes, stirring frequently until very soft.

Add the cream and bring to the boil, stirring. Simmer until slightly thickened. Season to taste. Cool slightly, then purée in a liquidiser (blender) or food processor. Pass through a fine sieve, if wished.

GREEN OLIVE DIP

1 tablespoon olive oil
2 tablespoons finely chopped shallots
1 clove of garlic, crushed
200g/7oz/1¹⁄₃ cups green olives, stoned (pitted)
250ml/8fl oz/1 cup chicken or vegetable stock
120ml/4fl oz/¹⁄₂ cup crème fraîche
juice of ¹⁄₂ lime
salt and freshly milled pepper

Heat the oil in a wide saucepan and sweat the shallots until translucent. Add the garlic and cook for a further minute.

Chop the olives very finely and add to the shallots. Add the stock and simmer, uncovered, for about 20 minutes until all the liquid has evaporated.

Stir in the crème fraîche and lime juice and simmer until the mixture thickens. Season to taste. Serve warm or cold.

CALF'S LIVER WITH SAGE ON FRENCH TOAST

Liver and sage must be one of the most successful food combinations ever conceived. Serve these canapés when you want something a bit more substantial than usual.

MAKES 10

2 eggs
2 tablespoons freshly grated Parmesan cheese
10 slices of baguette
75g/3oz/6 tablespoons unsalted butter
50ml/2fl oz/¼ cup olive oil
200g/7oz calf's liver
20 fresh sage leaves
salt and freshly milled pepper

Beat the eggs and Parmesan cheese together and season well. Dip the bread slices in the mixture.

Heat 50g/2oz/¼ cup of the butter and the oil in a large frying pan and fry the bread slices until golden brown on both sides. Keep warm.

Cut the calf's liver in 10 even-sized pieces. Heat half the remaining butter in a frying pan and quickly fry the liver on both sides. Season with salt and pepper and place a piece on each bread slice.

Heat the remaining butter in the frying pan and add the sage leaves. Remove from the pan immediately, top each piece of liver with two sage leaves and serve warm.

**QUICK AND SIMPLES
CALF'S LIVER WITH SAGE ON
FRENCH TOAST**

QUICK AND SIMPLES

Quick and Simples are the quintessential canapés of this chapter. In the recipe we mention fillet of beef, salmon and scallops. However, any tender meat leftovers such as chicken breast, lamb fillet and some white fish, such as brill, can be used. The ketchup and horseradish topping adds a brilliant contrast.

These canapés should be only lightly cooked; even the fish should always have a raw centre.

MAKES 30

150g/5oz fillet of beef
150g/5oz skinless and boneless fillet of salmon
5 large scallops without roe
30 thin slices of baguette
8 tablespoons tomato ketchup
4 teaspoons freshly grated horseradish
50g/2oz/¼ cup unsalted butter
salt and freshly milled pepper

Cut both the beef and salmon in ten even-sized pieces to fit the bread slices. Cut each scallop in half.

Toast the bread slices lightly on both sides and keep warm.

Place the tomato ketchup and horseradish in a small saucepan and heat gently. Spread a little on each piece of toasted bread.

Season the beef and fish with salt and pepper. Melt one-third of the butter in a frying pan and fry the beef quickly on both sides ensuring that it remains rare. Melt the remaining butter in another frying pan and fry the salmon and scallops very quickly on both sides.

Place a piece of meat or fish on each slice of toasted bread and serve at once.

CRUSTED CAMEMBERT

The warm mildness of Camembert together with the sharp freshness of cranberries is a titillating experience.

MAKES 30

1 Camembert cheese
2 tablespoons plain (all-purpose) flour
3-4 eggs, beaten
225-300g/8-10oz/4½-5½ cups fresh white breadcrumbs
oil for deep frying
cranberry sauce to serve

Cut the Camembert cheese in 30 small wedges and turn in the flour until evenly coated. Dip each wedge in beaten egg, then coat in breadcrumbs. Repeat the egg and breadcrumb coating once more.

Heat the oil and deep fry the wedges until crisp and golden. Drain on absorbent paper and spoon a small amount of cranberry sauce on each one. Press a cocktail stick (toothpick) in each one and serve at once.

SAVOY BACON MUFFINS

An invention of one of Anton's famous predecessors, possibly to serve with afternoon tea.

MAKES ABOUT 30

50g/2oz/3 slices streaky bacon, cut in fine julienne
50g/2oz/¼ cup unsalted butter
25g/1oz/¼ cup button mushrooms, diced
150g/5oz/1¼ cups self-raising flour
1 tablespoon freshly chopped herbs such as chives, parsley and basil
25g/1oz/2 tablespoons tomato fillet, diced
50g/2oz/scant ½ cup Gruyère cheese, grated
1 egg
100ml/3½fl oz/scant ½ cup milk
salt and freshly milled pepper

Blanch the bacon in boiling water, then drain thoroughly and fry in 1 teaspoon of the butter until crisp. Add the diced mushrooms and fry for a further 2 minutes until the mushrooms are golden and the liquid has been absorbed. Leave to cool.

Sift the flour into a bowl and rub in the remaining butter. Add the bacon and mushroom mixture, the herbs, tomato and half the cheese. Beat the egg and milk together, season generously and stir into the flour mixture until evenly combined.

Place 2 teaspoons of the mixture into greased miniature muffin tins and then sprinkle with the remaining cheese. Bake in a preheated oven at 220°C/425°F/gas mark 7 for about 15 minutes until risen and golden. Serve at once.

CRISP COURGETTES (ZUCCHINI) WITH PESTO

An unusual canapé with the flavours and aromas of Italy. It needs last-minute preparation.

MAKES ABOUT 40

300g/10oz/8-10 miniature courgettes (zucchini)
120ml/4fl oz/½ cup milk
50-75g/2-3oz/5 tablespoons-½ cup plain (all-purpose) flour
oil for deep frying
4-6 tablespoons pesto (see page 135)
25g/1oz/5 tablespoons Parmesan cheese, freshly grated
salt and freshly milled pepper

Cut the courgettes in slices about 5mm/¼ inch thick. Dip them in milk and then turn them in flour until evenly coated.

Heat the oil and deep fry the courgette slices in batches until crisp and golden. Drain on absorbent paper.

Place on a baking tray and spread with pesto. Sprinkle with the Parmesan cheese and brown quickly under a preheated grill (broiler).

PARMA PLUMS

Almost an Italian version of Devils on Horseback. Fresh dates make a delicious alternative to plums.

MAKES 20

10 ripe plums
100g/4oz Ricotta cheese
10 slices of Parma ham (prosciutto)
oil for deep frying

Halve and stone (pit) the plums. Place a small amount of cheese on each plum. Cut each slice of ham in half and wrap a piece around each piece of plum. Secure with a wooden cocktail stick (toothpick).

Heat the oil and fry the plums until the ham is golden brown. Drain on absorbent paper. Serve warm.

WELSH LAMB PICKUPS

MAKES 20

20 thin slices of baguette
unsalted butter for spreading
175g/6oz smoked lamb, thinly sliced
2 shallots or baby (pearl) onions, very thinly sliced
40 capers
salt and freshly milled pepper

Spread the bread thinly with butter.

Cut the lamb in strips and arrange on the bread. Top each canapé with a few onion rings and two capers. Season to taste.

PUFFS

Originally from Spain and Portugal, where they are eaten before lunch or dinner with dry sherry or white port.

Manchego cheese is a popular Spanish hard cheese. Cheddar or Gruyère may be substituted.

MAKES ABOUT 30

40g/1½oz/3 tablespoons unsalted butter
120ml/4fl oz/½ cup milk
¼ teaspoon salt
65g/2½oz/7 tablespoons plain (all-purpose) flour, sifted
2 eggs, beaten
50g/2oz/½ cup Manchego cheese, grated
4 tablespoons pine kernels
½ teaspoon Dijon mustard
oil for deep frying
paprika

Place the butter, milk and salt in a saucepan and bring to the boil. Off the heat, beat in the flour until the mixture forms a ball. Beat in the eggs a little at a time, then stir in the cheese, pine kernels and mustard.

Heat the oil and deep fry teaspoonfuls of the mixture over a medium heat for about 5 minutes until crisp and golden. Drain on absorbent paper and dust with paprika.

SALAMI TOMATOES

These should be served to clear the palate and add a hint of sweetness to the menu.

MAKES 30

30 cherry tomatoes
100g/4oz/½ cup good quality salami, minced (ground)
1 teaspoon capers, chopped
1 teaspoon finely chopped spring onion (scallion)
1 tablespoon finely chopped gherkins
25g/1oz/1½ tablespoons stoned (pitted) green olives, finely chopped

Slice the tops off the tomatoes and discard the seeds. Turn the tomatoes upside down on a kitchen cloth (dish towel) to drain.

Combine the remaining ingredients until evenly mixed and use to fill the tomatoes.

SWISS BEEF CORNETS

The Swiss have every right to be proud of their air-dried beef with its unique flavour. Although this combination of pâté and meat is particularly good, try experimenting with the wonderful assortment of charcuterie available in most delicatessens and supermarkets, to make a whole range of savoury cornets.

MAKES 20

*20 paper-thin slices of viande de grisson
(air-dried Swiss beef)
100g/4oz/1/2 cup smooth chicken liver pâté
6 slices of dark rye bread
unsalted butter for spreading
20 small slices of mango
sage leaves and pistachio nuts to garnish*

Remove the rind from the slices of dried beef and roll each one in a cornet shape.

Soften the pâté and using a piping bag fitted with a small star nozzle (tube), pipe a whirl of pâté into each cornet.

Spread the bread lightly with butter and stamp out 20 4cm/1½ inch diamonds from the bread. Arrange a slice of mango on each one and top with a cornet shape.

Garnish with pistachio nuts and sage leaves.

VALENTINE CANAPÉS

Invented for Valentine's Day, these heart-shaped croûtons, with two half quails' eggs sitting on top to form a heart within a heart, are sadly not an aphrodisiac.

MAKES 20

*20 small heart-shaped pieces of thinly
sliced bread
oil for deep frying
100g/4oz/1/2 cup soft white cheese
2 tablespoons chopped chives
20 quails' eggs
Beluga caviar
Keta caviar
20 corn salad hearts (lamb's lettuce)
sauce vierge (see page 135)
dill to garnish (optional)*

Deep fry the heart-shaped pieces of bread in hot oil until crisp and golden. Drain on absorbent paper.

Combine the soft cheese and chives and spread thinly on the hearts.

Cook the quails' eggs in boiling salted water for 1½ minutes, drain and refresh in iced water. Remove the shells from the eggs and cut each one in half. Place two halves on each heart and garnish one half with a little Beluga caviar and the other with Keta caviar.

Arrange the corn salad between the halves of egg and garnish with a little sauce vierge and dill, if wished.

BRESSE BLEU WITH TRUFFLES

If truffle is unavailable or you're feeling poor, garnish each canapé with a piece of roasted pecan nut! Bresse bleu is quite the best cheese for this recipe, but also try adapting it using other soft cheeses, with or without vein.

MAKES 20

*5 slices of rye bread
unsalted butter for spreading
two 125g/4½oz boxes Bresse bleu cheese
20 half-slices of truffle*

Spread the bread generously with butter. Using a 4cm/1½ inch cutter, stamp out four rounds from each slice.

Cut each Bresse bleu cheese in ten thin slices and using the cutter, make each one the same size as the bread. Place one slice of cheese on each round of bread. Garnish each one with a slice of truffle.

**VALENTINE CANAPÉS
SWISS BEEF CORNETS
BRESSE BLEU WITH TRUFFLES**

CROQUE MONSIEUR

An all-time French favourite which fits in surprisingly well – especially with a glass of red wine! A more complex version involves making a sandwich with the ham and cheese, dipping it in beaten egg flavoured with Parmesan cheese, and frying until crisp and golden.

MAKES ABOUT 20

8 thin slices of white bread from a large loaf
unsalted butter for spreading
4 teaspoons whole-grain mustard
100g/4oz cooked ham, thinly sliced
100g/4oz/1¼ cups Gruyère cheese, grated

Toast the bread lightly, then remove the crusts. Spread the toast with butter and then with a little mustard.

Divide the ham between four slices of the toast and sandwich together with the remaining slices. Press down firmly. Sprinkle the top of each sandwich with cheese and cook under a preheated grill (broiler) until the cheese is bubbling.

Cut each sandwich in six pieces and serve warm.

MINTED MELON BALLS

Refreshing on a sunny day – ideal before a barbecue or garden party.

Any type of melon will do as long as it is really ripe. The melon balls may be prepared and stored in the refrigerator for several hours but do not wrap in ham until required as the juices cause the meat to 'weep'.

MAKES 40

900g/2lb ripe melon – choose from honeydew,
Charentais or Ogen
2 tablespoons finely chopped mint
10 thin slices of Parma ham (prosciutto)

Cut the melon in half and discard the seeds; then scoop out about 20 balls from each half of the melon, using a parisian cutter. Alternatively, cut cubes of melon.

Drain the melon balls thoroughly on a kitchen cloth (dish towel) then roll in the freshly chopped mint.

Cut each slice of ham in four lengthways and wrap a piece around each melon ball. Secure with a cocktail stick (toothpick).

AVOCADO, TOMATO AND BASIL CRACKERS

MAKES 20

2 plum tomatoes
1 ripe avocado
40 leaves of fresh basil
lemon juice
salt and freshly milled pepper
20 savoury round biscuits such as Ritz crackers

Blanch, peel and remove the seeds from the tomatoes and cut in fine dice. Remove the stone (pit) from the avocado, then peel and cut in fine dice. Chop half the basil leaves.

Combine four-fifths of the tomato with the avocado and chopped basil. Season with lemon juice, salt and pepper to taste.

Spoon a little mixture on to each cracker and garnish with a basil leaf and the remaining diced tomato.

OYSTER MUSHROOMS
FILLED WITH
MOZZARELLA AND BASIL

MAKES 20

20 small oyster mushrooms
2 tablespoons vegetable oil
2 tablespoons extra virgin olive oil
½ teaspoon balsamic vinegar
1 teaspoon finely chopped shallot
¼ clove of garlic, crushed
1 plum tomato, peeled, seeds removed
and diced
1 tablespoon freshly chopped basil
salt and freshly milled pepper
40g/1½oz/¼ cup Mozzarella cheese, cut in
tiny dice
20 small squares of olive bread, toasted

Clean the mushrooms thoroughly. Heat
a little of the vegetable oil in a frying pan
(skillet) and very quickly cook a few
mushrooms at a time, adding more oil as
necessary. Cool on a wire tray.

Mix together the olive oil and vinegar,
then add the shallot, garlic, tomato and
basil. Season to taste.

Season the mushrooms and place a few
dice of Mozzarella on each one. Glaze
under a preheated grill. Top with a small
amount of the tomato and basil mixture
and place each one on a piece of toasted
bread.

SMOKED EEL
WITH PAPAYA

Always choose baby eel, either smoked
or fresh, as it has the most delicate taste
and texture. It makes an interesting
alternative to the much more popular
smoked salmon.

MAKES 40

1 ripe papaya
1 crisp dessert apple such as a Granny Smith
2 celery sticks
20g/¾oz/2 tablespoons chopped
hazelnuts, toasted
1 teaspoon freshly grated horseradish
50ml/2fl oz/¼ cup of crème fraîche
25ml/1fl oz/2 tablespoons mayonnaise
(see page 137)
salt and freshly milled pepper
200g/7oz smoked baby eel
40 small squares of rye bread
unsalted butter for spreading
chopped chives to garnish

Halve, remove the seeds and peel the
papaya, then cut in half lengthways. Cut
each quarter in 10 thin slices.

Quarter, peel, core and dice the apple.
Peel the coarse strings from the celery
and cut in small dice. Mix the apple,
celery, hazelnuts, horseradish, crème
fraîche and mayonnaise together and
season to taste.

Cut the eel in 40 thin slices. Spread the
bread lightly with butter and arrange a
piece of eel and a slice of papaya on each.
Top with a little apple and celery mixture
and sprinkle with chopped chives.

MINTED CREAM CHEESE
WITH HAZELNUTS

MAKES 20

4 slices of wholemeal (wholewheat) bread
100g/4oz/½ cup cream or curd cheese
15g/½oz/1 tablespoon chopped hazelnuts,
roasted
25g/1oz/2 tablespoons Parma ham
(prosciutto), chopped
20 mint leaves, chopped
20 celery leaves
20 whole hazelnuts, roasted
8 fresh lychees, skinned and sliced

Toast the bread, then stamp out 20
4cm/1½ inch rounds.

Combine the cheese, chopped hazelnuts, ham and mint. Arrange a celery leaf
on each round of bread and spoon a little
of the cheese mixture on top. Garnish
each one with a whole hazelnut and some
slices of lychee.

MUSHROOM AND RADISH WHIRLS

HEALTHY

A N D

Wise

'Never trust a thin chef,' a client at The Savoy once said. But eating well does not mean eating vast quantities; it simply means having a well-balanced diet of different foods cooked in many different ways. It does not take twentieth-century science and over-indulgence to realise that too much of a good thing leads not to a gourmet's delight, but to a gourmand's early grave – or at least to a minor heart attack.

All religions recognised this at an early stage. There is Lent in the Christian belief, Ramadan amongst the Muslims and lengthy fasting periods in the Jewish faith. Indeed, in most cultures there seems to be a code of how to eat and how much to eat, and after a great feast there should always be a day of fasting. 'Never trust a fat chef' would perhaps be a wiser maxim!

Here are two delicious non-alcoholic
drinks which have been specially created
by Peter Dorelli, Head Barman of
The Savoy.

PREVENTION

50ml/2fl oz/¼ cup passion fruit nectar
50ml/2fl oz/¼ cup cranberry juice
25ml/1fl oz/2 tablespoons orange juice
25ml/1fl oz/2 tablespoons grapefruit juice
25ml/1fl oz/2 tablespoons apple juice
fresh banana
3 dashes of gomme syrup

Blend the ingredients together with ice
and decorate with slices of orange and
lime, a cherry and a sprig of mint.

HEALTHLINER

50ml/2fl oz/¼ cup apple juice
25ml/1fl oz/2 tablespoons fruit nectar
25ml/1fl oz/2 tablespoons cranberry juice
3 fresh strawberries
½ fresh peach
coconut cream
fresh cream

Blend with ice and decorate with
strawberries and kiwi.

MUSHROOM WHIRLS

A great canapé for those who like to stay slim and trim, easy to eat, with an intensity of natural flavours. They can be kept in the refrigerator under clingfilm for several hours without deteriorating.

Other vegetables such as celeriac, parsnip, artichoke heart, swede (rutabaga), kohlrabi, pea or broad bean, can replace the carrots. Vandyked large radishes may be used instead of the mushrooms.

MAKES 20

5 large carrots (about 600g/1½lb)
25g/1oz/2 tablespoons unsalted butter
salt and freshly milled pepper
20 medium-sized button mushrooms
sprigs of fresh herbs

Peel and trim the carrots. Cut in even-sized pieces and steam or cook in boiling salted water until very tender. Drain thoroughly.

Purée the carrots, then pass through a fine sieve. Beat in the softened butter and season generously with salt and pepper.

Remove the stalks from the mushrooms and peel off the outer skin. Using a piping bag fitted with a medium star nozzle (tube), pipe the carrot purée into the mushroom cups. Garnish each one with a tiny sprig of fresh herb.

PHOTOGRAPH ON PAGE 26

LENTIL BURGERS

Lentils and other pulses often form the staple diet of a nation providing necessary protein, but in Britain we often tend to associate such foods with vegetarianism and consequently malign them. A lot of people underestimate the lentil.

Lentil de puy is the 'king' of lentils so make it your first choice.

MAKES ABOUT 40

225g/8oz/1 cup green lentils
50g/2oz/½ cup onion, roughly chopped
1 clove of garlic, bruised
1 small bay leaf
40g/1½oz/2½ tablespoons each of leek, celery
and carrot, cut in tiny dice and blanched
1 egg yolk
2 tablespoons freshly chopped tarragon
salt and freshly milled pepper
vegetable oil
tomato relish to serve

Soak the lentils in cold water for 1 hour. Drain and place in a saucepan with the onion, garlic and bay leaf and cover with cold, salted water.

Bring to the boil, then simmer for about 20 minutes until the lentils are tender, adding extra water if necessary. Drain thoroughly.

Divide the cooked lentils equally and work one half in a food processor with the garlic and onion. Mix in the remaining lentils, vegetables, egg yolk and tarragon. Season to taste. Form the mixture into little burgers.

Heat a minimum of vegetable oil in a non-stick frying pan and brown the lentil burgers quickly on both sides. Serve with a little tomato relish on top.

BABY AVOCADOS

Miniature avocados are available early in the year – they are sausage shaped, unlike the classic avocado, because the stone has not developed properly. They are ideal to use as canapés. Just like the classic avocado they must be ripe to give their best flavour and texture.

MAKES 20

10 ripe baby avocados
lemon juice
chilli sauce (optional)
100g/4oz/½ cup cottage cheese
40g/1½oz/⅓ cup mango, sliced
40g/1½oz/⅓ cup papaya, sliced
40g/1½oz/⅓ cup kiwi, sliced
20 sprigs of mint

Cut the avocados in half, peel and remove the undeveloped stones (pits). Brush with lemon juice and then a little chilli sauce, if wished.

Spoon a little cottage cheese on to each avocado and top with a small amount of fruit. Garnish each one with a sprig of mint.

MANGETOUT (SNOW PEA) BOATS

An uncomplicated little canapé which is easy to eat. The crunchiness of the green pod and the soft sharpness of the cheese complement each other perfectly.

MAKES 40

40 mangetout (snow peas) or sugar snap peas
100g/4oz Roquefort cheese, sieved
100g/4oz/½ cup low-fat soft cheese
½ red (sweet) pepper, peeled and finely diced

Remove the stalks from the mangetout or sugar snap peas and blanch for 2-3 seconds. Drain and refresh in iced water. Drain thoroughly. Open each mangetout or sugar snap pea along one side using a small sharp knife.

Mix together the Roquefort and soft cheese. Using a piping bag fitted with a small star nozzle (tube), pipe a little cheese into each mangetout or sugar snap pea.

Garnish with a sprinkling of diced red pepper.

CELERY BARQUETTES

You can use any cheese which is soft or blue-veined as a filling for these barquettes. Scoops of soft Brie are delicious but if you're really weight-watching use a very low-fat cheese such as Quark.

MAKES ABOUT 30

200g/7oz blue or white Stilton cheese
50g/2oz/¼ cup unsalted butter, softened
1 head of celery
peeled walnut pieces to garnish

Place the Stilton cheese and butter in a food processor and work until very smooth.

Using a vegetable peeler, peel the celery to remove any coarse strings on each stalk. Leave any small leaves in place. Cut the celery in 10cm/4 inch lengths.

Using a piping bag fitted with a small star nozzle (tube), pipe a short length of the Stilton mixture into each celery barquette. Garnish with pieces of walnut.

HELLENIC ARTICHOKES

It is quite a lot of work to prepare fresh artichokes, but the result is so worthwhile and their unique flavour so different from anything that comes out of a can.

It is sometimes possible to buy miniature globe artichokes. If available, prepare them in the same way but cook for only 2-3 minutes.

MAKES 10

10 globe artichokes
lemon juice
350g/12oz/1½ cups hummus or taramasalata
2-3 spring onions (scallions), finely sliced

Break off the stalks from the artichokes. Using a very sharp knife, cut off all the large leaves at the base leaving a cone of soft small leaves in the centre of each artichoke.

Trim the artichoke bottoms evenly. Cut off the soft cone of leaves and carefully scrape away the 'choke' from each artichoke. Brush with lemon juice frequently during this preparation to prevent discolouration.

Cook the artichoke bottoms in boiling salted water for 7 minutes until just tender. Drain and refresh in iced water. Drain thoroughly.

Fill the artichoke bottoms with hummus or taramasalata and sprinkle each one with a little spring onion.

CELERY BARQUETTES
MANGETOUT (SNOWPEA) BOATS

FANTASY OF SMOKED SALMON

This recipe was first developed for a small wedding party where the bride was particular about her food. She ate this as a canapé, then also had it as a starter. She has been coming back to The Savoy for her wedding anniversary dinner for the last 6 years and always asks for the same starter!

MAKES 30

175g/6oz smoked salmon, thinly sliced
225g/8oz/1 cup curd cheese
4 tablespoons chopped chives
30 slices of cucumber
Keta caviar to garnish

Lay half the smoked salmon out to make a rectangle about 30 × 10cm / 12 × 4 inches, overlapping the slices as necessary. Repeat with the remaining smoked salmon.

Beat together the curd cheese and chives and use to fill a piping bag fitted with a 2cm/¾ inch plain nozzle (tube). Pipe half the mixture along one long side of each rectangle of smoked salmon, then roll up the salmon to enclose the mixture. Chill the roulades for at least 1 hour.

Cut each roulade in 15 pieces and place each one on a slice of cucumber. Top with a little Keta caviar.

SEABASS FLUTES

Small individual fennel leaves should ideally be used as a base for this canapé, in which case buy the smallest possible fennel. Separate the leaves from the bulb and cook for about 5 minutes until just tender but still crunchy, otherwise the fennel will be too soft to pick up.

The intense aniseed flavour of the fennel combines so well with fish.

MAKES 20

2 Florence fennel bulbs, each weighing about 225g/8oz
200g/7oz seabass fillet, skin and bones removed
50g/2oz/scant ½ cup Gruyère cheese, grated
salt and freshly milled pepper
sauce vierge (see page 135)

Remove the fennel fronds from the top of each fennel bulb and reserve. Discard the outer leaf of the fennel bulbs and using a vegetable peeler, peel the bulbs to remove any stringy bits.

Cook the fennel in a steamer or in boiling salted water for about 15 minutes until just tender. Drain and cool.

Season the seabass with salt and pepper and steam for 5 minutes. Cut in 20 small pieces. Cut each fennel bulb, through the root, in five slices, discarding the rounded-end pieces. Cut each slice in half.

Lay the pieces of fennel on a lightly oiled baking tray and place a piece of seabass on each. Sprinkle with a little Gruyère and place under a preheated grill (boiler) at the hottest setting to just melt the cheese.

Spoon a little sauce vierge on to each portion and garnish with a fennel frond. Serve warm.

CUCUMBER TEASERS

A light and refreshing little canapé ideal to eat on a warm summer's day.

MAKES ABOUT 20

1 cucumber
120ml/4fl oz/½ cup strained Greek yoghurt
1 small clove garlic, crushed
4 radishes, finely chopped
salt and freshly milled pepper
sprigs of dill to garnish

Using a canneling knife, remove strips of peel along the length of the cucumber to give a decorative effect. Cut about 20 1.5cm/½ inch slices from the cucumber and scoop out most of the seeds with a teaspoon, leaving a thin layer to act as a base.

Peel the remaining cucumber, discard the seeds and cut in very fine dice. Combine with the yoghurt, garlic and radishes. Season to taste. Spoon a little of the mixture into each cucumber 'cup' and garnish with a sprig of dill.

ORCHESTRA OF VEGETABLES WITH DIPS

An arrangement of beautifully prepared fresh vegetables which looks so attractive that it's just as likely to be used as a table decoration. Nothing looks fresher and more appetising than the natural beauty and varying colours of this carefully arranged selection. Hard-boiled quail's or gull's eggs, halved and sprinkled with celery salt or oriental salt, are a good addition.

Choose organically grown vegetables where possible as they are usually more intense in taste and colour. The rule is to provide plenty of everything – always ensure that the dips are strong in taste and well seasoned so that they form a contrast to the vegetables.

Choose the vegetables from the following suggestions:

Miniature vegetables with their green tops left on where appropriate:
> *kohlrabi*
> *carrots*
> *radishes cut in flowers*
> *yellow and red cherry tomatoes*
> *sweetcorn*
> *button mushrooms*
> *sugar snap peas*
> *mangetout (snow peas)*

Florets of romanesque (green) or
> *white cauliflower*

Batons of:
> *carrot*
> *cucumber*
> *kohlrabi*
> *celery*

Leaves of Belgian endive (chicory)

AUBERGINE (EGGPLANT) DIP

1 large aubergine (eggplant)
1 small clove of garlic
3/4 teaspoon salt
1 tablespoon tahini (sesame paste)
1 tablespoon lemon juice
1/2 teaspoon ground cumin
1 1/2 teaspoons olive oil
1 tablespoon freshly chopped parsley
pinch of chilli powder

Wash the aubergine and cut a few slits in it with a sharp knife. Place on a baking tray and bake in a preheated oven at 190°C/375°F/gas mark 5 for about 30 minutes until the skin is black and the aubergine is soft.

Cut the aubergine in half and scoop out the flesh. Place it in a food processor with the remaining ingredients and blend until smooth.

AVOCADO AND FROMAGE FRAIS DIP

1 ripe avocado
250g/9oz/heaped 1 cup low-fat fromage frais
1 small clove of garlic, crushed
1 teaspoon lemon juice
1/2 teaspoon chilli oil
salt

Halve, stone (pit) and peel the avocado and place in a food processor or liquidiser (blender) with the remaining ingredients. Work to a smooth consistency and season to taste with salt.

TOMATO AND BASIL DIP

2 tablespoons olive oil
50g/2oz/1/3 cup onion, finely chopped
1 clove of garlic, crushed
300g/10oz/2 cups plum tomatoes, peeled, seeds removed and sliced
120ml/4fl oz/1/2 cup vegetable stock
2 teaspoons freshly chopped basil
salt and freshly milled pepper

Heat the oil and sweat the onions until translucent, then add the garlic and cook for a further minute.

Add the tomatoes and stock and simmer for about 10 minutes until the mixture is thick. Stir in the basil and season to taste. Serve at room temperature and not chilled.

KIDNEY BEAN DIP

100g/4oz/3/4 cup kidney beans
1/2 onion, chopped
2 cloves of garlic, crushed
2 chillies, sliced
6 tablespoons tomato ketchup
salt

Soak the kidney beans for 8-12 hours. Drain and rinse thoroughly.

Cook the beans in boiling salted water for 45 minutes, then add the onion, garlic and chillies and simmer for a further 45 minutes.

Drain, reserving the cooking liquid. Blend the beans in a food processor, then add the ketchup and a little reserved cooking liquid if necessary to produce the required consistency. Pass through a fine sieve and season to taste with salt.

FRESH FIG, CHEESE AND STRAWBERRY BISCUITS

This is a very pretty canapé which the ladies love.

Make absolutely sure that the figs are of the best possible quality – they need to be very ripe and sweet to get the best results. Keep blanched shreds of orange rind in a jar of sugar syrup.

MAKES 30

8 ripe fresh figs, peeled
30 small savoury round biscuits such as Ritz crackers
100g/4oz/¹/₂ cup curd cheese
4 large strawberries
30 small mint leaves
shreds of orange rind to garnish

Cut four slices from the centre of each fig. Place a slice of fig on each biscuit.

Using two teaspoons, shape 30 tiny quenelles of curd cheese and place one on top of each slice of fig. Cut the strawberries in wedges and press one or two pieces of strawberry and a mint leaf into each cheese quenelle. Garnish with orange rind. Serve cool but not chilled.

FRESH FIG, CHEESE AND STRAWBERRY BISCUITS
COCKTAIL TOMATOES
KIWI BITES

COCKTAIL TOMATOES

At The Savoy we use organically grown cherry tomatoes from California which are so sweet in taste that you can smell the scent of the intense sun which has ripened them.

In the height of their season they are good enough to eat on their own with a tiny dash of salt or quickly dipped in vodka and then lightly dipped in a good quality curry powder.

MAKES 50

25 red cherry tomatoes
25 yellow cherry tomatoes
40g/1½oz/3 tablespoons white crab meat
½ small avocado, finely diced
1 tablespoon finely diced tomato fillet
1 tablespoon finely diced cucumber without skin or seeds
1 tablespoon freshly chopped coriander (cilantro)
2 tablespoons mayonnaise (see page 137)
50g/2oz/3 tablespoons peeled cooked prawns (shrimp), diced
¼ small green (sweet) pepper, skinned and diced
¼ small red (sweet) pepper, skinned and diced
50g/2oz/3 tablespoons celery, skinned and diced
1 teaspoon freshly chopped chives
lemon juice
salt and freshly milled pepper
chives or herb sprigs to garnish

Cut the top off each tomato and carefully take out the seeds and any pulp to leave a hollow shell. Turn the tomatoes upside down on absorbent paper and leave to drain.

Mix together the crab meat, avocado, tomato, cucumber, coriander and half the mayonnaise. Season to taste with lemon juice, salt and pepper. Use to fill the red tomatoes.

Mix together the prawns, green and red peppers, celery, chives and remaining mayonnaise. Season to taste with lemon juice, salt and pepper. Use to fill the yellow tomatoes.

Garnish all the tomatoes with small lengths of chive or herb sprigs in the top of each one.

KIWI BITES

Quick and easy to prepare – a good standby canapé.

MAKES 30

4 kiwi fruit, peeled
8 slices of rye bread
unsalted butter for spreading
200g/7oz/heaped ¾ cup low-fat soft cheese
1 plum tomato, blanched, peeled and seeds removed
dill sprigs to garnish

Cut each kiwi fruit in eight even slices.

Spread the bread with a thin scraping of butter, then stamp out 30 4cm/1½ inch rounds.

Place a slice of kiwi fruit on each round of bread. If wished, the fruit may be cut to the exact size of the bread using the same cutter.

Using two teaspoons, shape 30 tiny cheese quenelles and place one on each slice of kiwi fruit. Cut 30 tiny pieces of tomato and place one on top of each cheese quenelle. Garnish with dill sprigs.

SALMON CARPACCIO

A delicate and light dish which takes careful preparation and presentation, but brings out the flavour of the salmon beautifully.

MAKES ABOUT 30

350g/12oz salmon fillet, skinned and boned
salt and freshly milled pepper
juice of 1 lemon
4 tablespoons olive oil
1 teaspoon green peppercorns, finely crushed
1 teaspoon coriander seeds, finely crushed
2 tablespoons freshly chopped coriander
(cilantro)
9 slices of pumpernickel
unsalted butter for spreading
30 coriander (cilantro) leaves to garnish

Cut the salmon in about 30 very thin slices and lay out on a plastic tray. Season with salt and pepper.

Combine the lemon juice, olive oil, peppercorns, coriander seeds and chopped coriander and use to marinate the salmon. Cover and leave in a cool place for at least 15 minutes or up to 4 hours.

Spread the pumpernickel with a thin scraping of butter, then stamp out small rounds – about 5cm/2 inches in diameter.

Fold each piece of salmon in a rosette and place on top of the pumpernickel. Garnish each one with a coriander leaf.

MEDITERRANEAN PATTYPAN SQUASH

Cannoise, similar to ratatouille, is an ideal filling for these baby squash or other baby vegetables of your choice.

MAKES 20

10 baby yellow squash, blanched
10 baby green squash, blanched
1 small onion, finely chopped
25g/1oz/2 tablespoons unsalted butter
2 tablespoons olive oil
2 cloves of garlic, crushed
3 plum tomatoes, skinned, seeds removed
and diced
½ red (sweet) pepper, skinned and diced
½ green (sweet) pepper, skinned and diced
1 small yellow courgette (zucchini), diced
1 small green courgette (zucchini), diced
20g/¾oz/2 tablespoons Parmesan cheese, grated
salt and freshly milled pepper

Cut a 'lid' from the top of each squash and reserve. Scoop out the middle of each one to make a cup. Place on a buttered baking tray.

Sweat the onion in the butter and oil until translucent, then add the garlic and sweat for a further minute.

Add the tomatoes, peppers and courgettes, season with salt and pepper and simmer gently until *al dente*. Use the mixture to fill the squash, then sprinkle with Parmesan cheese.

Place in a preheated oven at 220°C/425°F/gas mark 7 for about 5 minutes to heat through. When the cheese is slightly coloured, place the 'lids' on top and heat for a further 1-2 minutes. Serve at once.

PEPPERED MUSSELS

Make sure the mussels are really fresh for this canapé. The natural shells make ideal serving cups, but do balance them on a bed of sea salt or seaweed to stop them wobbling on the plate.

MAKES ABOUT 20

450g/1lb mussels
120ml/4fl oz/½ cup dry white wine
2 cloves of garlic, chopped
freshly milled pepper
1-2 teaspoons lemon juice
¼ small green (sweet) pepper, skinned and cut
in tiny dice
¼ small yellow, red or orange (sweet) pepper,
skinned and cut in tiny dice
freshly chopped parsley

Scrub the mussel shells thoroughly and discard any open ones. Remove the beards.

Heat the wine, garlic and a grinding of pepper in a saucepan and add the mussels. Cover and cook over a high heat for 2-3 minutes until the shells open. Drain, reserving the juices. Remove and discard the half shells.

Strain the pan juices through muslin (cheesecloth), then boil to reduce to 3-4 tablespoons. Season with lemon juice and pepper. Then brush over the mussels to glaze. Sprinkle with the finely diced peppers and a little chopped parsley.

CHICKEN AND LEEK ROULADES WITH LIME AND ORANGE SAUCE

This is quite an ambitious 'spoon' canapé which takes some time to prepare, but is well worth the effort.

Serve the slices on medium spoons, and arrange the spoons on a dish or plate.

MAKES ABOUT 20

3 175g/6oz skinless and boneless chicken breasts
40g/1½oz/3 tablespoons unsalted butter
1 tablespoon vegetable oil
25g/1oz/3 tablespoons onion, finely chopped
1 clove of garlic, crushed
½ teaspoon finely grated lime rind
½ teaspoon freshly grated root ginger
25g/1oz/2½ tablespoons nibbed almonds
100g/4oz/½ cup chicken mousse (see page 134)
3 miniature leeks
chicken stock
40g/1½oz/2 tablespoons caster sugar
2 tablespoons Curaçao or Grand Marnier
3 tablespoons lime juice
120ml/4fl oz/½ cup orange juice
1 teaspoon arrowroot powder
salt and freshly milled pepper

Using a sharp knife, cut almost through each chicken breast from the side and open it out like a butterfly. Place between two sheets of plastic film and beat out until thin and evenly flattened. The feather fillets from each chicken breast should be detached and flattened separately. Season with salt and pepper.

Heat 10g/¼oz/½ tablespoon of the butter and the oil and sweat the onion until translucent, then add the garlic and cook for a further minute. Stir in the grated lime rind, ginger and almonds and leave to cool. Add to the chicken mousse and season generously.

Cut the white part of the leeks to the same length as the chicken breasts and blanch in boiling salted water for 3-4 minutes. Drain and refresh in iced water, then dry thoroughly on a kitchen cloth (dish towel).

Spread the chicken mousse mixture over the three chicken breasts, leaving a clean edge around each one.

Lay a piece of leek in the centre of each and top with the flattened feather fillet. Roll up the chicken breasts to completely enclose the leek; then wrap each one securely in cling film.

Place the chicken roulades in a saucepan and just cover with boiling chicken stock. Simmer for 12 minutes, then drain and leave to cool for 10 minutes.

Place the remaining butter and sugar in a small saucepan and cook over a medium heat until the sugar caramelises. Remove from the heat and carefully add the Curaçao. Stir in the lime juice and three-quarters of the orange juice. Bring to the boil and reduce by half by fast boiling.

Mix the arrowroot powder with the remaining orange juice and stir into the sauce. Cook, stirring, until thickened.

Unwrap the chicken roulades and cut each one in neat slices. Arrange the slices in spoons and pour a little sauce on each one. Alternatively, serve the slices on a plate with the sauce served separately for dipping.

BELGIAN ENDIVE (CHICORY) SPIKES

Belgian endive is undoubtedly a favourite; the bitterness of the vegetable married with either something sweet or slightly salty produces a heavenly taste.

MAKES 30

300g/10oz/1¼ cups soft cheese, flavoured with garlic and herbs
30 small Belgian endive (chicory) leaves, trimmed
75g/3oz smoked salmon, cut in julienne

Beat the cheese until smooth, then place in a piping bag fitted with a star nozzle (tube) and pipe some on to each endive leaf. Top with smoked salmon julienne.

LOBSTER WITH ASPARAGUS

LUXURIOUS

AND

Extravagant

There are times when we all dream of having a really luxurious party – a costly affair with all the trimmings – maybe to celebrate a special occasion, to spoil a few friends, or quite simply as a purely personal indulgence!

For many of us, lobster, caviar, langoustines and foie gras are not foods which can be readily found in the fridge. However, for a cocktail party, you do not need vast quantities of these exceptional, and of course, very expensive items – you can still impress with small amounts. Two Black Sea Blinis, or two or three Goose Liver Pâté Eclairs are quite enough to serve per person, assuming that your guests will appreciate such delicate little mouthfuls.

Mix and match is the answer, so make two or three items from the luxurious and extravagant collection and then add a selection from other chapters to balance the diet, and the purse. There are some menu ideas on page 140 – so bon appetit!

CELEBRATION

A wonderful Champagne cocktail
created by Peter Dorelli, Head Barman at
The Savoy.

⅗ brandy
⅕ Benedictine
⅕ crème de mure

Shake with ice and top up with
Champagne.
Serve in frosted glasses.

LOBSTER WITH ASPARAGUS

It is very important to make this canapé as late as possible so that the lobster medallions keep their fresh appearance. Dried lobster eggs are used to garnish at The Savoy. To dry the eggs, spread the cooked eggs on a baking tray and place in the oven set at a low temperature.

MAKES 10

2-3 slices rye or brown bread
unsalted butter for spreading
assorted salad leaves
1 cooked lobster tail, shell removed
10 tiny asparagus tips, cooked al dente
cocktail sauce (see page 136)
10 sprigs of chervil
dried lobster eggs (optional)

Spread the bread with butter and cut out ten 5cm/2 inch squares. Place tiny pieces of salad leaves on each.

Cut the lobster tail in ten medallions and place on top of the leaves.

Cut the asparagus tips in half lengthways and arrange on top.

Using a greaseproof (wax) paper piping bag, pipe a tiny drizzle of cocktail sauce over each canapé and garnish with a chervil leaf and a few dried lobster eggs, if wished.

PHOTOGRAPH ON PAGE 38

SMOKED DUCK ON RYE

The inhabitants of Gascogne in south-west France, and of the Bordeaux region, believe that the duck is a saintly animal. Every part of the duck gets used from the deliciously rich liver to the skin – which is often crispy fried as in this recipe where it gives such a contrasting texture.

MAKES ABOUT 30

1 smoked duck or goose breast weighing about
225g/8oz
4 tablespoons vegetable oil
1 teaspoon clear honey
1 teaspoon lime juice
½ loaf of rye bread
unsalted butter for spreading
1 small ripe mango
6 radishes,
thinly sliced
1 small head Belgian endive (chicory), thinly
sliced
salt and freshly milled pepper

Remove the skin from the duck or goose breast and cut in 5mm/¼ inch dice. Heat 3 tablespoons of the oil and quickly fry the duck skin until very crisp. Drain on absorbent paper.

Mix together the remaining oil, honey and lime juice and season with salt and pepper. Spread the bread with butter and stamp out 6.5cm/2½ inch rounds.

Thinly slice the duck or goose. Peel the mango, remove the stone (pit) and cut the fruit in thin slices.

Mix the crispy skin with the radishes and Belgian endive and moisten with the dressing. Spoon a little on each piece of bread, then arrange the duck or goose and mango slices on top.

MOSCOVITE POTATOES

These delightful little potatoes topped with caviar are probably at their best when the new Jersey potatoes come into season. The tax haven of Jersey and caviar seem to go well together!

MAKES 20

20 small new potatoes weighing about 40g/
1½oz each
100g/4oz sea salt
4 tablespoons soured cream
2 tablespoons chopped chives
50g/2oz/3 tablespoons Beluga or Keta caviar

Scrub the potatoes thoroughly under running water.

Arrange the sea salt in a baking tin and place the potatoes on top. Bake in a preheated oven at 200°C/400°F/gas mark 6 for about 45 minutes until tender.

Brush all the salt carefully from the potatoes and cut a cross in the top of each one. Press the potatoes to open out the cross.

Mix the soured cream with the chives and spoon a little on to each potato. Place a generous helping of caviar on each one and serve at once.

BELGIAN OYSTERS

The world is divided into those with a passion for oysters 'au naturel' or for their delicate flavour when lightly cooked.
Oysters used to be part of the staple diet of the poor people in Britain but sadly they have become an expensive item on the menu. Hopefully with the advent of farmed rock oysters this need not be so any more, as they are now available all year round at increasingly affordable prices.

MAKES 30

30 Pacific oysters
10 spinach or sorrel leaves, blanched
about 300ml/1/2 pint/1 1/4 cups Noilly Prat
for poaching
plain (all-purpose) flour for dusting
beer batter (see page 79)
oil for deep frying
30 large leaves Belgian endive (chicory),
trimmed to an even size, or use the rounded half
of the oyster shell
lemon juice for sprinkling
10 teaspoons rémoulade sauce (see page 136)
parsley sprigs, deep fried until crisp
25g/1oz/1 1/2 tablespoons Beluga caviar
25g/1oz/1 1/2 tablespoons Keta caviar

To remove the oysters from their shells: hold the flat side uppermost firmly with a cloth, hinged end towards you and insert a short, wide-bladed knife under the hinge, then twist the knife to separate the shells sliding it along the upper shell to release the muscle. Loosen the oysters from the under shell and remove the beards. Wrap ten oysters in the spinach leaves and poach for 30 seconds in the Noilly Prat. Remove from the pan and keep warm. Dust another ten with flour, dip in beer batter and deep fry in hot oil until crisp and golden. Keep warm.

Sprinkle the Belgian endive leaves with lemon juice. Place a small spoonful of rémoulade sauce on the wide end of ten of the leaves and top with a fried oyster and fried parsley. Place the raw oysters on ten of the leaves and top each with a little Beluga caviar. Place the wrapped oysters on the remaining leaves and top each with a little Keta caviar. Serve at once.

BELGIAN OYSTERS
WILD RICE PANCAKES

WILD RICE PANCAKES

Wild rice, often called 'vegetarian caviar', has a delicate but particular flavour which mixes well with other rices and in egg dishes such as these tiny pancakes.

Choose all sorts of other toppings – both savoury and sweet – to add variety to your cocktail party menu.

MAKES ABOUT 20

50g/2oz/5 tablespoons plain (all-purpose)
flour, sifted
1 egg
4 tablespoons milk
200g/7oz/1 1/3 cups cooked wild rice
2 tablespoons freshly chopped chives
salt and freshly milled pepper
unsalted butter or vegetable oil for frying

Mix the flour, egg and milk together until smooth, then stir in the wild rice and chives and season generously with salt and pepper.

Heat a little butter or oil in a large frying pan or griddle and drop tablespoonfuls of the mixture on to the pan. Flatten lightly with the back of a spoon. Cook until golden brown on both sides. Serve topped with:
Parma ham (prosciutto) and melon: Cut tiny slices of melon and arrange on top of the pancakes with pieces of Parma ham, strawberry and sage leaves.
Smoked salmon julienne with creamed horseradish: Mix together 120ml/4fl oz/ 1/2 cup double (heavy) cream with 25g/ 1oz/3 tablespoons grated horseradish (or more to taste). Cut 200g/7oz smoked salmon in julienne strips and arrange on the pancakes. Garnish with creamed horseradish and dill sprigs.

GOOSE LIVER PÂTÉ ECLAIRS

Goose liver almost forms part of a Frenchman's religion, and eaten in moderation for special occasions it is something absolutely wonderful. You will never forget the creamy texture.

MAKES ABOUT 40

2 egg quantity choux paste (see page 138)
beaten egg
finely chopped pistachio nuts to sprinkle
225g/8oz/1cup goose liver pâté
75g/3oz/6 tablespoons unsalted butter
brandy (optional)

Using a piping bag fitted with 1cm/⅜ inch plain nozzle (tube), pipe short lengths of choux paste on a lightly greased baking tray. Brush with beaten egg and sprinkle with chopped pistachio nuts. Bake in a preheated oven at 220°C/425°F/gas mark 7 for 10-15 minutes until crisp and golden. Make a small incision in each one to allow the steam to escape. Cool on a wire tray.

Pass the goose liver pâté through a fine sieve. Beat the butter until smooth, then mix in the pâté. Flavour with brandy to taste, if wished.

Cut each eclair in half and using a piping bag fitted with a star nozzle, fill each eclair with a little pâté.

TIGER PRAWNS (SHRIMP) IN BATTER JACKETS

Another import from a trip to Thailand where Tiger prawns seem to be juicier, bigger and better than anywhere else.

MAKES 40

40 raw Tiger prawns (shrimp)
150ml/¼ pint/⅔ cup olive oil
1 clove of garlic, crushed
1 tablespoon light soy sauce
oil for deep frying
For the batter:
225g/8oz/scant 2 cups plain (all-purpose) flour
pinch of salt
6 tablespoons olive oil
350ml/12fl oz/1½ cups tepid water
pinch of cayenne
2 egg whites

Carefully remove the shells from the prawns, leaving the tails intact. Cut along the length of each back and remove the intestine. Wash and dry thoroughly.

Place the Tiger prawns in a bowl and add the olive oil, garlic and soy sauce. Cover and leave to marinate in a cool place for up to 24 hours.

For the batter, sift the flour and salt into a bowl. Beat in the olive oil and water to give a smooth batter. Season with a little cayenne.

Drain the prawns thoroughly and start to heat the oil for deep frying.

Whisk the egg whites until stiff with a pinch of salt, then fold into the batter. Dip the prawns in the batter, holding them by the tails, then drop into the hot oil. Cook until crisp and golden. Drain on absorbent paper. Serve at once.

JAPANESE MUSHROOM CUPS

This Japanese dressing was developed at The Savoy. It has an intriguing and unusual flavour which mixes well with almost any salad.

MAKES 40

40 medium-sized very fresh button mushrooms
200g/7oz/1½ cups peeled cooked prawns (shrimp), roughly chopped
½ quantity Japanese dressing (see recipe below)
small amount of fine julienne of carrot, kohlrabi and courgette (zucchini) skin to garnish

Mix the prawns in the dressing and use to fill the mushroom cups. Top with a tiny amount of vegetable julienne.

JAPANESE DRESSING

8 teaspoons red wine vinegar
2 teaspoons Dijon mustard
½ clove of garlic, crushed
3 tablespoons caster (superfine) sugar
Worcestershire sauce
Tabasco sauce
50ml/2fl oz/¼ cup olive oil
5 teaspoons soy sauce
5 teaspoons tomato ketchup
40g/1½oz/2 tablespoons leek and carrot, cut in tiny dice and blanched
salt and freshly milled pepper

Whisk the vinegar, mustard, garlic and sugar together. Add a dash of Worcestershire and Tabasco sauces, then whisk in the olive oil, soy sauce and tomato ketchup. Stir in the diced vegetable and season to taste.

SCOTTISH TREATS

MAKES 20

175g/6oz brioche dough (see page 68)
unsalted butter for spreading
1 large ripe mango, peeled and thinly sliced
175g/6oz/1 cup cooked lobster meat, chopped
50ml/2fl oz/¼ cup crème fraîche
1 tablespoon chopped chives
5ml/1 teaspoon lemon juice
salt and pepper
sprigs of chervil

On a lightly floured surface, roll out the brioche paste thinly. Place on a lightly greased baking tray (sheet) and leave to prove for 20 minutes. Bake in a preheated oven at 220°C/425°F/gas mark 7 for about 10 minutes until golden brown. Leave to cool.

Spread the brioche with butter, then stamp out 30 4cm/1½ inch rounds. Stamp out 30 4cm/1½ inch rounds of mango and place one on each piece of brioche.

Chop any remaining mango and mix with the lobster, crème fraîche, chives and lemon juice and season to taste. Spoon a little of the mixture on top of each slice of mango and garnish with a sprig of chervil.

NEW YORK CRAB CAKES

MAKES 10

200g/7oz/1½ cups white crab meat
2 tablespoons mayonnaise
20g/¾oz/1½ tablespoons gherkins,
finely chopped
20g/¾oz/1½ tablespoons celery, finely chopped
Tabasco sauce
beaten egg for coating
100g/4oz/2 cups fresh white breadcrumbs, sieved
120ml/4fl oz/½ cup fish stock
120ml/4fl oz/½ cup dry white wine
250ml/8fl oz/1 cup double (heavy) cream
1½ teaspoons whole-grain mustard
2 tablespoons freshly chopped herbs such as
chervil, coriander (cilantro) and parsley
1 teaspoon capers, finely chopped
salt and freshly milled pepper
oil for deep frying

Mix together the crab meat, mayonnaise, gherkins and celery. Season with a few drops of Tabasco sauce, salt and pepper.

Divide the mixture in ten portions and shape each one into a ball. Dip each ball in beaten egg and then coat in the fresh breadcrumbs until evenly covered. Place on a baking tray and flatten each one slightly to make small cakes.

Reduce the fish stock and white wine by two-thirds by fast boiling. Add the cream and reduce by one-third until the sauce coats the back of a spoon. Stir in the mustard, herbs and capers and season to taste. Keep warm.

Heat the oil and fry the crab cakes until crisp and golden. Drain on absorbent paper.

Serve the crab cakes at once with the sauce served separately as a dip.

LANGOUSTINE POUCHES

MAKES ABOUT 20

For the omelettes:
6 eggs
6 tablespoons iced water
1 tablespoon freshly chopped parsley
salt and freshly milled pepper

For the filling:
10 langoustines, steamed and shelled
50g/2oz/½ cup mangetout (snow peas)
50g/2oz/⅓ cup carrot
50g/2oz/⅓ cup beansprouts
50ml/2fl oz/¼ cup olive oil
25ml/1fl oz/2 tablespoons soy sauce
1 teaspoon caster (superfine) sugar
1 tablespoon freshly chopped chives
20 long chives, blanched

For the omelettes, beat the eggs and water together with the parsley and season generously with salt and pepper.

Lightly oil a 15cm/6 inch diameter frying pan and place over a medium heat. Pour sufficient egg batter into the pan to just cover the base and cook until just set. Remove from the pan and lay out on a flat surface. Repeat the process until all the batter is used up and there are about 20 omelettes.

Roughly chop the langoustines. Cut the vegetables in short julienne. Mix together the olive oil, soy sauce, sugar and chopped chives. Fold in the langoustines and vegetables. Season to taste.

Place a small amount of filling on each omelette and draw in the sides to make a pouch. Secure with a long chive and trim off the excess omelette above the tie.

GOURMET DELIGHT

This has to be tasted to be appreciated!

MAKES 10

150g/5oz fillet of beef
1 egg yolk
2 teaspoons finely chopped onion
1 teaspoon capers, chopped
1 teaspoon chopped gherkin
2 anchovy fillets, chopped
4 tablespoons freshly chopped parsley
paprika
Tabasco
Worcestershire sauce
brandy
salt and freshly milled pepper
3-4 slices of white bread
2 tablespoons vegetable oil
25g/1oz/2 tablespoons unsalted butter
10 quails' eggs
10 sprigs of chervil

Chop the fillet of beef very finely, then add the egg yolk, onion, capers, gherkin, anchovy and 1 tablespoon of the parsley. Mix well and season to taste with paprika, Tabasco, Worcestershire sauce, brandy, salt and pepper.

Cut 5cm/2inch rounds from the bread. Heat the oil and butter in a frying pan and fry the bread in batches until crisp and golden. Turn the edges in the remaining parsley until evenly coated.

Divide the beef in ten equal portions and shape each one to fit on top of a round of fried bread. Make a small dip in the top of each one.

Separate the egg yolks from the quails' eggs and place a yolk on each portion. Garnish with a sprig of chervil.

BLACK SEA BLINIS

Many things have been said about caviar, including the fact that it is overrated and too expensive but it is especially delightful when served on warm blinis. It's definitely the high point of a special party.
There are many types of caviar to choose from so it doesn't have to be Beluga all the time – Sevruga is considerably cheaper, and Oscietra is a good quality product at about a fifth of the price of Beluga.
For a special effect, cook large blinis and stamp out small rounds with a fluted cutter.

MAKES 40

For the batter:
120ml/4fl oz/½ cup milk
1 teaspoon fresh yeast
2 eggs, separated
¼ teaspoon salt
¼ teaspoon caster (superfine) sugar
2 tablespoons melted butter
65g/2½oz/½ cup buckwheat flour
40g/1½oz/¼ cup plain (all-purpose) flour
unsalted butter for frying

For the garnish:
unsalted butter
hard-boiled egg
freshly chopped parsley
finely chopped onion
Beluga caviar
crème fraîche or soured cream
chives

For the batter, heat the milk to lukewarm, add the yeast and stir until evenly mixed. Beat the egg yolks and add the yeast liquid, salt, sugar and melted butter. Combine the flours and beat in the liquid to give a smooth batter. Whisk the egg whites until stiff and fold into the batter.

Lightly butter a griddle and preheat to medium heat. Place 1½ teaspoons batter on the griddle to make each pancake. Cook until bubbles appear on the surface and the mixture has started to set then turn and cook until golden on the other side. Repeat until all the mixture is used. Alternatively, make large blinis and stamp out small rounds with a fluted cutter.

Spread the blinis generously with butter and keep warm.

Separate the hard-boiled eggs into yolk and white and pass separately through a fine sieve.

Arrange some egg yolk, egg white, parsley and onion on each blini to completely cover one quarter of the surface each. Pipe dots of crème fraîche around the edge and one in the centre, then garnish with caviar and chives.

Alternatively, serve the blinis plain and all the garnishes in small dishes so that guests can add their own toppings.

CARPACCIO
GOURMET DELIGHT
BLACK SEA BLINIS

CARPACCIO

The original carpaccio comes from the Cipriani Hotel in Venice where it was created by Guiseppe Cipriani for the launch of an exhibition of Carpaccio's paintings.

It's much easier to start with a larger piece of fillet of beef and cut the paper-thin slices you require from it.

Wrap the beef in a kitchen (dish) cloth and secure with string. Chill as required then carve off wafer-thin slices with a very sharp knife.

MAKES 20

175g/6oz raw fillet of beef
4 tablespoons olive oil
4 teaspoons lemon juice
salt and freshly milled pepper
20 small pieces of ciabatta (Italian bread), toasted
tiny leaves of spinach or rocket
25g/1oz/5 tablespoons Parmesan cheese
truffle oil (optional)

Cut the beef in 20 paper-thin slices and arrange on a flat serving dish or tray. Drizzle with the oil and lemon juice and season generously.

Place a slice of beef on each piece of ciabatta and top each with 4-5 spinach leaves and a shaving of Parmesan cheese. Drizzle with a little truffle oil, if wished.

PHOTOGRAPH ON PAGE 47

MINI PRALINES OF FOIE GRAS

This elaborate canapé epitomises the Périgueux region of France where goose liver is combined with truffles. A simpler version may be made omitting the quails' eggs and simply shaping the pâté, then continuing with the recipe below.

MAKES 20

100g/4oz/1 cup truffles, finely chopped
10 quails' eggs
150g/5oz/²⁄₃ cup pâté de foie gras
500ml/18fl oz/2¼ cups duck aspic (see page 135)
3-4 miniature brioches
a few leaves of curly endive (chicory)
a few leaves of lollo rosso

Lay the truffles out on a baking tray and dry them slowly in a warm place such as an airing cupboard or the warming drawer of the oven.

Cook the quails' eggs in boiling salted water for 2 minutes, then refresh in iced water. Remove the shells and dry the eggs on a kitchen cloth (dish towel).

Mould a little pâté carefully around each egg. Chill in the refrigerator until firm, then roll each one in chopped truffles until evenly coated.

Melt half the aspic and chill it just to the consistency of unbeaten egg white. Chill the remaining aspic until set, then chop it finely.

Carefully cut the eggs in half and place them on a wire tray over a plastic tray. Spoon a little aspic over each one to glaze it. Chill the eggs for a few minutes, then glaze with the aspic once more. Chill until set.

Thinly slice the brioches and toast. Stamp out a 6cm/2½ inch round from each slice. Top each slice of brioche with a small amount of salad leaves. Place a glazed egg on each slice and pipe a small amount of the chopped set aspic around each one, using a greaseproof (wax) paper piping bag.

SMOKED SALMON DREAMS

MAKES 20

150g/5oz shortcrust pastry (see page 138)
50ml/2fl oz/¼ cup crème fraîche
50g/2oz/4 tablespoons Beluga caviar
50g/2oz smoked salmon slices
20 sprigs of dill

On a lightly floured surface, roll out the pastry as thinly as possible and use to line 20 2.5-4cm/1-1½ inch tartlet tins (pans). Leave to rest in a cool place for at least 20 minutes, then bake blind in a preheated oven at 200°C/400°F/gas mark 6 for about 10 minutes until golden brown. Leave to cool, then remove from the tins.

Mix the crème fraîche with the caviar and use to fill the pastry tartlets. Stamp out 20 2.5-4cm/1-1½ inch rounds of smoked salmon and place one on top of each tartlet. Garnish each one with a sprig of dill.

QUAILS' EGG TARTLETS WITH TRUFFLE BUTTER

Truffle juice is made by marinating fresh truffles in port (see Périgueux Indulgence page 105).

MAKES 20

15g/¹/₂oz/1 tablespoon unsalted butter
50g/2oz/¹/₃ cup leek, cut in very small dice
20 quails' eggs
20 miniature shortcrust pastry tartlets
truffle butter (see below)

Melt the butter and sweat the leek until tender.

Cook the quails' eggs in boiling salted water for 1½ minutes. Refresh in iced water, then carefully peel away the shells.

Place a small amount of leek in each tartlet case and place a quail's egg on top. Spoon a little truffle butter over each egg and serve at once.

TRUFFLE BUTTER

50ml/2fl oz/¹/₄ cup balsamic vinegar
50ml/2fl oz/¹/₄ cup sherry vinegar
50ml/2fl oz/¹/₄ cup ruby port
50ml/2fl oz/¹/₄ cup truffle juice
50ml/2fl oz/¹/₄ cup double (heavy) cream
65g/2¹/₂oz/heaped ¹/₄ cup unsalted butter
cayenne salt

Place the vinegars, port and truffle juice in a small saucepan and reduce by three-quarters by fast boiling.

Stir in the cream and reduce to a thick syrupy consistency. Remove from the heat and work in the butter a little at a time. Season with salt and cayenne.

SALMON IN A PASTRY TRELLIS

Technically, this is quite difficult to prepare but can be made the day before, ready to bake at the last moment, and serve with a glass of crisp dry white wine – it guarantees a gasp among your guests!

Trellis cutters are available from specialist kitchen shops – the rotating wheel cuts through the pastry making it into a decorative lattice.

MAKES ABOUT 30

50g/2oz/4 tablespoons combined leek, carrot and kohlrabi, finely diced and blanched
225g/8oz/1 cup fish mousse (see page 134)
6 egg-white pancakes (see page 99)
150g/5oz salmon fillet, cut in strips about 1cm/³/₈ inch wide
salt and freshly milled white pepper
175g/6oz puff pastry
beaten egg to glaze

Dry the vegetables thoroughly on a kitchen cloth (dish towel), then combine with the fish mousse and season generously.

Lay three pancakes in a line so that they overlap. Trim off the rounded edges. Spread half the fish mousse mixture across the centre of the pancakes leaving a small border all the way round. Place half the salmon strips along the length of the mousse. Roll up the pancakes carefully to enclose the filling. Repeat with the remaining pancakes to make a second roll.

On a lightly floured surface, roll out the pastry thinly. It should be a little longer than the pancake roll and wide enough to wrap around both rolls. Cut the pastry in half. Using a trellis cutter, mark out a lattice on each piece of pastry. Use the pastry to completely enclose the pancake rolls, sealing the edges well with beaten egg. Place on a lightly greased baking tray and leave to rest in a cool place for at least 20 minutes.

Brush with beaten egg and bake in a preheated oven at 220°C/425°F/gas mark 7 for 20-25 minutes until golden brown. Allow to cool for about 5 minutes, then cut in slices to serve.

PHOTOGRAPH ON PAGE 51

CORIANDER (CILANTRO) CRISPS WITH KIDNEY

Filo pastry is enjoying ever-increasing popularity in the modern
kitchen because of its light crisp texture.
The Savoy kitchens import the finest quality French filo pastry.
Unfortunately, it is not available over the counter yet, so use one of the
Greek pastries available.
Sweetbreads may be used instead of kidneys.

MAKES 30

4 large sheets of filo pastry
1 egg
4 tablespoons double (heavy) cream
60 coriander (cilantro) leaves
oil for deep frying
25g/1oz/2 tablespoons unsalted butter
50g/2oz/⅓ cup leeks, cut in tiny dice
1 teaspoon English (dry) made mustard
4 lamb's kidneys
1 tablespoon vegetable oil
salt and freshly milled pepper

Stamp out 120 4cm/1½ inch rounds from
the sheets of filo pastry. Mix the egg
with 1 tablespoon of the cream and brush
over the pastry rounds. Sandwich two
pastry rounds together with a coriander
leaf in between and press well to seal.
Make a few pin pricks in each one to
prevent them blistering when fried.

Deep fry the coriander discs until crisp
and golden. Drain on absorbent paper.

Melt half the butter, sweat the leeks,
add the remaining cream and mustard
and cook until thickened. Season to taste.

Halve the kidneys and remove the
cores. Season with salt and pepper. Heat
the remaining butter and oil and cook the
kidneys until browned on all sides. Cut
in thin slices.

Spoon a little leek on to half the
coriander discs and top each one with
some slices of kidney and a second
coriander disc.

SALMON IN A PASTRY TRELLIS
JACKETED LAMB
CORIANDER (CILANTRO) CRISPS WITH KIDNEY

JACKETED LAMB

MAKES 20

2 best ends of lamb (rack roasts)
2 tablespoons vegetable oil
100g/4oz/½ cup chicken mousse (see page 134)
50g/2oz/¼ cup carrot purée (see page 135)
8 egg-white pancakes (see page 99)
75g/3oz/1 cup tender spinach leaves, blanched
salt and freshly milled pepper
175g/6oz puff pastry
beaten egg to glaze

Remove all the bones and fat from the lamb, leaving the fillets. Season each fillet with salt and pepper. Heat the oil in a frying pan and seal the two pieces of lamb very quickly on all sides. Leave to cool.

Combine the chicken mousse and carrot purée and season generously.

Lay four egg-white pancakes slightly overlapping to form a square. Trim the edges. Dry the spinach leaves thoroughly and lay half of them in a single layer on the pancakes. Spread evenly with half the chicken mousse mixture. Place a cold lamb fillet in the centre and fold the pancakes over to form a parcel. Repeat with the second fillet.

On a lightly floured surface, roll out the pastry very thinly and mark out a lattice with a trellis cutter. Cut the pastry in half and completely enclose each lamb fillet, sealing the edges well with a little beaten egg. Leave to rest in a cool place for at least 20 minutes.

Place on a lightly oiled baking tray, brush with beaten egg to glaze and bake in a preheated oven at 230°C/450°F/gas mark 8 for 10 minutes. Leave to rest for 15 minutes, then cut in slices to serve.

MUSHROOM CUPS FILLED WITH CRABMEAT

MAKES 20

20 medium-sized mushroom cups
50ml/2fl oz/¼ cup vegetable or olive oil
1 tablespoon chopped shallot
½ clove of garlic, crushed
½ red pepper, skinned and diced
½ green chilli, skinned and diced
100ml/3½fl oz/scant ½ cup white crabmeat
150ml/¼ pint/⅔ cup Béchamel sauce
(see page 137)
40g/1½oz/⅓ cup Emmenthal cheese, grated
1 egg yolk
2 tablespoons double (heavy) cream, whipped
salt and freshly milled pepper

Remove the stems from the mushroom cups and wash and dry thoroughly. Heat 2 tablespoons of the oil and toss the mushrooms quickly. Season to taste.

Heat the remaining oil and sweat the shallots until translucent. Add the garlic and sweat for a further minute. Add the diced pepper and chilli and sweat for a further minute. Stir in the crabmeat and about three-quarters of the Béchamel sauce to bind the mixture together. Season to taste. Use to fill the mushroom cups, then sprinkle with half the cheese.

Add the remaining cheese, the egg yolk and cream to the remaining sauce. Season to taste and spoon a little over each mushroom. Glaze under a preheated grill (broiler) and serve at once.

SALMON TARTARE ON RYE

The salmon has to be very fresh for this recipe so that it will take on the character of each ingredient added. Salmon tartare should have the taste of the sea from the sea salt, a touch of sweetness from the sugar, and a tang of bitterness from the lemon. The cheese or crème fraîche should not take away the edge of those three ingredients but contribute to their harmony.

MAKES ABOUT 30

400g/14oz salmon fillet, skinned and boned
50g/2oz/½ cup sea salt
15g/½oz/2 teaspoons caster (superfine) sugar
¼ teaspoon saltpetre (potassium nitrate)
juice of ½ lemon
8-10 slices of rye bread
unsalted butter for spreading
200g/7oz/scant 1 cup curd cheese or crème fraîche
4 teaspoons finely chopped chives

Wash the salmon fillet, then dry it on a kitchen cloth (dish towel).

Mix together the salt, sugar and salt-petre. Cover the salmon fillet evenly with this mixture, cover and leave to marinate in the refrigerator for 3 hours. Wash off the salt mixture and dry the fillet of salmon on a kitchen cloth. Cover and leave in the refrigerator for a further 3 hours.

Spread the bread with butter and stamp out 5cm/2 inch rounds.

Finely chop the salmon and mix with the lemon juice. Place the cutter over a round of bread and press a small amount of the salmon tartare neatly on top.

Repeat with the remaining rounds of bread and salmon tartare.

Mix the curd cheese and chives and spread a little on top of each round of salmon. If using crème fraîche, it is a good idea to make these in moulds. Spoon the crème fraîche on top of the salmon and chill in the refrigerator for at least 1 hour until set. Carefully remove the moulds, if using.

NORI SEAWEED SUSHI WITH JAPANESE RADISH

Seaweed sushi is traditionally rolled on a bamboo mat. Cucumber or smoked or raw fish may be used to replace the Japanese radish.

MAKES 20

2 sheets of dried Nori seaweed
175g/6oz cooked sushi rice (see next recipe)
1 teaspoon Japanese horseradish powder
mixed to a paste with warm water
2 teaspoons toasted sesame seeds
15g/½ oz/4 teaspoons Japanese pickled ginger
50g/2oz/⅓ cup Japanese fresh yellow radish,
cut in julienne
Japanese soy sauce for dipping

Place the dried seaweed on a bamboo mat. Arrange the rice in a line about 2.5cm/1 inch wide close to one edge of the seaweed. Indent the rice along its length, dot with the horseradish paste and sprinkle with the sesame seeds. Lay the Japanese ginger on top in a single layer and top with the Japanese radish.

Roll the seaweed around the rice using the bamboo mat to give an even cylindrical shape. Cut with a very sharp knife in thin slices.

Serve with soy sauce handed separately for dipping.

SALMON SUSHI THE EASY WAY

I first discovered sushi many years ago but it only became one of my most favourite dishes after my first trip to Japan nearly three years ago. Since then I have begun to appreciate all aspects of Japanese food.

Sushi is very exciting, healthy, nourishing and extremely colourful. It can only be made with local fish which must always be very fresh.

The following recipe is not suitable for shellfish with the exception of scallops.

Sushi is fun to prepare and eat at home especially if you serve it with Japanese green tea or warmed Saki.

MAKES 20

150g/5oz fresh salmon fillet (or any other
native fish)
225g/8oz cooked sushi rice (see recipe below)
20g/¾oz/2 tablespoons Japanese pickled ginger
1 teaspoon Japanese horseradish powder mixed
to a paste with warm water
Japanese soy sauce for dipping

For the sushi rice:
175g/6oz/1 cup Japanese short-grain rice
250ml/8fl oz/1 cup water
2.5cm/1 inch piece of kelp
40ml/1½fl oz/3 tablespoons rice vinegar
1½ teaspoons salt
½ teaspoon caster (superfine) sugar

Place the salmon fillet in iced water and leave for 1 hour. Remove and dry thoroughly on a kitchen cloth (dish towel).

Meanwhile, wash the rice in several changes of water until the water becomes clear. Place the rice and measured water in a heavy-based saucepan. Wash the kelp and add to the rice. Cover and simmer until all the water has evaporated, then leave to rest for 10 minutes.

Warm the rice vinegar, add the salt and sugar and stir until dissolved. Remove the kelp from the rice and stir in the vinegar mixture. Leave to cool.

Divide the cooked rice into 20 equal portions and shape each one in a cylindrical form. Dot a small amount of horseradish on top of the rice, then lay a single piece of pickled ginger on top.

Cut the salmon in very thin slices about 3mm/⅛ inch thick and slightly larger than the rice cylinders. Place carefully on top of the rice. Serve at once with the soy sauce handed separately for dipping.

MARINATED SCALLOPS WITH CAVIAR

TRADITIONAL

A N D

Trendy

A lot has been said about fashion in food, and whilst food cannot escape this comment, it is probably worthwhile remembering our roots and the old values of tried and proven methods. Indeed, looking closer at very many food items which are heralded as different, as new, one cannot help getting a feeling of déjà-vu.

The new very often evolves from the old and well known, and there's nothing wrong with that. Sausage rolls, for instance, are nowadays transformed in to small elegant nutty tasting canapés but nothing can hide the fact that they are hundreds and hundreds of years old and in fact a completely traditional food. In some ways this is very reassuring.

Already in 1734 there was a French chef called Laurent Dumas who published a book called *La Nouvelle Cuisine*, which does tend to put everything nowadays into perspective:

'As I always say, nothing is really new, it has all been done before. New trends and fashions in foods mean only that we improve on the taste, the quality of the produce and polish the presentation of what in many ways we have already done before.'

REFLEXION

A long refreshing mixer specially created
for this chapter by Peter Dorelli,
Head Barman at The Savoy.

⅖ vodka
⅕ cointreau
⅖ lime juice
gomme syrup
white of egg

Shake with ice and top up with soda.
Decorate with a slice of lime and a sprig
of mint.

MARINATED SCALLOPS WITH CAVIAR

A dream canapé – marinated scallops topped with Beluga caviar and flavoured with lime juice, a mouth-watering combination.

MAKES 20

4-5 large scallops without roe
juice of 1 lime
50ml/2fl oz/¼ cup olive oil
½ teaspoon green peppercorns, crushed
salt and freshly milled pepper
5 slices of rye bread
unsalted butter for spreading
Beluga caviar
20 small sprigs of chervil

Trim the scallops, the cut each one in 4-5 even slices and place on a plate in a single layer.

Mix the lime juice, oil and seasonings and pour over the scallops. Cover and marinade in the refrigerator for at least 15 minutes or up to 4 hours.

Spread the bread with butter and stamp out 20 rounds the same size as the scallops. Place a slice of scallop on each piece of bread. Garnish with a small amount of caviar and a sprig of chervil shaped to represent a bunch of grapes.

PHOTOGRAPH ON PAGE 54

THEARNE EGGS

Simply the best stuffed eggs ever made!

MAKES 20

10 small free-range eggs
50g/2oz/¼ cup unsalted butter
1 shallot, finely chopped
100g/4oz/½ cup peeled cooked prawns
(shrimp), roughly chopped
150ml/¼ pint/⅔ cup white wine sauce
(see page 136)
1 tablespoon freshly chopped basil
salt and freshly milled pepper
40g/1½oz/¾ cup brioche crumbs or fresh
breadcrumbs
20 small basil leaves to garnish

Cook the eggs in boiling salted water for 10 minutes. Drain and refresh in iced water, then remove the shells. Cut each egg in half lengthways and carefully remove the yolk. Pass the yolk through a fine sieve.

Melt a quarter of the butter and sweat the shallot until translucent. Add the prawns, white wine sauce and basil. Stir in the egg yolk. Season to taste.

Fill the halved egg whites with the prawn mixture.

Melt the remaining butter in a small saucepan and cook the brioche crumbs or breadcrumbs until golden. Sprinkle a few over each egg half and garnish with a small basil leaf. Serve warm.

SALMON AND SESAME CROQUETTES

MAKES ABOUT 40

450g/1lb cooked fresh salmon
2 tablespoons mayonnaise (see page 137)
salt and freshly milled pepper
plain (all-purpose) flour
milk
sesame seeds
oil for deep frying
rémoulade sauce to serve (see page 136)

Remove any skin and bones from the salmon and flake the fish. Combine with the mayonnaise and season to taste.

Divide the mixture in about 40 even-sized portions and shape each one into a crescent. Chill thoroughly.

Dip the crescents in flour to coat them lightly, then dip quickly in milk and coat with sesame seeds. Chill until required.

Heat the oil over a medium heat and deep fry the salmon crescents. Drain on absorbent paper and serve warm with rémoulade sauce.

SALMON OATCAKES

A canapé using traditional Scottish ingredients which has recently been re-vamped to the delight of the clientele at The Savoy.

MAKES ABOUT 20

225g/8oz gravad lax, finely chopped
4 anchovy fillets, finely chopped
175g/6oz/³/₄ cup cooked potato, sieved
2 egg yolks
4 tablespoons mayonnaise (see page 137)
3 radishes (skin only), finely chopped
15g/¹/₂oz/¹/₄ cup fresh white breadcrumbs
2 teaspoons freshly chopped dill
2 tablespoons freshly chopped parsley
salt and freshly milled pepper
plain (all-purpose) flour
beaten egg
50g/2oz/3 heaped tablespoons medium oatmeal
clarified butter for frying
mustard sauce (see page 136)

Combine the gravad lax, anchovy fillets, potato, egg yolks, mayonnaise, radishes, breadcrumbs and herbs. Season to taste. Divide the mixture in about 20 small cakes. Dip in flour, beaten egg and finally oatmeal until evenly coated. Reshape as necessary.

Heat some clarified butter in a frying pan and shallow fry the salmon oatcakes until crisp and golden on both sides. Drain on absorbent paper. Serve warm with mustard sauce.

CARAMELISED APPLES WITH BLUE CHEESE

This little amusement was created at The Savoy for a dinner for caterers who drank unusual wines with unusual dishes, such as good claret with fish. It was served with Sauternes – Château d'Yquem 1976, a mere £240 per bottle – a delightful contrast to the sweetness of the apple and the sharpness of the Roquefort.

This canapé is photographed opposite with 'flowers' of Tête de Moine cheese encasing the crumbled Roquefort. The flowers are made with a special carousel cutter.

MAKES ABOUT 20

3 Golden Delicious dessert apples
lemon juice
icing (confectioners') sugar
vegetable oil for deep frying
225g/8oz Roquefort cheese, crumbled
50g/2oz/¹/₃ cup celery, finely diced
25g/1oz/¹/₄ cup shelled walnuts, finely chopped
celery leaves

Wipe the apples and cut each one in extremely thin rings. You should get 8-10 good slices per apple. Brush each slice with lemon juice and sprinkle generously with sifted icing sugar.

Heat the oil to medium heat and fry the apple slices very slowly until they turn an even golden colour. Place on a wire tray to cool. As they cool they will curl and become crisp.

Divide the cheese between the apple rings. Sprinkle the walnuts on top and garnish with celery leaves.

PIGLETS IN BLANKETS

The sophisticated sausage roll always delights guests when served warm from the oven.

MAKES ABOUT 40

15g/¹/₂oz/1 tablespoon unsalted butter
2 tablespoons finely chopped onion
225g/8oz good quality sausagemeat with herbs
25g/1oz/¹/₄ cup pistachio nuts, skinned
and chopped
225g/8oz puff pastry
beaten egg to glaze
fennel seeds, poppy seeds or sesame seeds to
sprinkle

Melt the butter and sweat the onion until translucent. Leave to cool. Combine the sausagemeat, onion and pistachio nuts.

Roll out the pastry on a lightly floured surface and cut out four strips each measuring 25 × 7.5cm/10 × 3 inches.

Roll the sausagemeat in four strips the same length as the pastry. Place a piece of sausagemeat on each strip of pastry and brush one long edge with a little beaten egg. Roll up to completely surround the sausagemeat and seal well. Place the rolls seam-side down, brush with beaten egg and sprinkle with fennel seeds. Cut into 2.5cm/1 inch lengths.

Place on a lightly buttered baking tray and bake in a pre-heated oven at 220°C/425°F/gas mark 7 for about 15 minutes until crisp and golden. Serve warm.

PIGLETS IN BLANKETS
CARAMELISED APPLES WITH
BLUE CHEESE

PARTY POTATOES

A wholesome canapé which might help to soak up the excesses of alcohol!

MAKES 30

30 new potatoes weighing 40-50g/1½-2oz each
4 tablespoons vegetable oil
50g/2oz/3 slices streaky bacon
6 eggs
2 tablespoons unsalted butter
4 tablespoons crème fraîche
2 tablespoons freshly chopped chives
75g/3oz smoked salmon, cut in fine julienne
salt and freshly milled pepper

Wash the potatoes thoroughly, then place in a roasting tin (pan) with 2 tablespoons of the oil. Shake well to coat the skins evenly. Bake in a preheated oven at 200°C/400°F/gas mark 6 for about 45 minutes until tender.

Remove the top of each potato and scoop out the inside to make firm containers. Finely dice the cooked potato.

Heat the remaining oil and fry the bacon and diced potato until crisp and golden. Drain on a kitchen cloth (dish towel).

Whisk the eggs and season with salt and pepper. Melt the butter in a non-stick pan and cook the eggs over medium heat until lightly scrambled. Remove from the heat and add the crème fraîche to prevent further cooking. Stir in the bacon mixture and chives and use to fill the potatoes.

Top with the smoked salmon julienne and serve at once.

EVESHAM CLUSTERS

Chicken and asparagus combines to make the ultimate vol-au-vents. Always serve them crisp and warm, there's nothing worse than cold soft puff pastry!

MAKES 40

20g/¾oz/1½ tablespoons unsalted butter
100g/4oz/1 cup button mushrooms, diced
120ml/4fl oz/½ cup dry white wine
200ml/7fl oz/scant 1 cup chicken stock
100g/4oz/½ cup skinless and boneless chicken breast
120ml/4fl oz/½ cup double (heavy) cream
40g/1½oz/⅓ cup asparagus spears, blanched and diced
salt and freshly milled pepper
40 cocktail vol-au-vent cases measuring about 4cm/1½ inches, baked

Heat the butter in a saucepan and sweat the mushrooms for 2 minutes. Add half the white wine and simmer for a further 2 minutes.

Remove the mushrooms from the saucepan and add the remaining wine. Reduce it by half by fast boiling, then add the chicken stock.

Poach the chicken breast in the stock for about 10 minutes until thoroughly cooked. Remove from the stock and leave to cool. Cut in small dice.

Reduce the cooking liquid by fast boiling, then add the cream and reduce to a coating consistency. Stir in the chicken, mushrooms and asparagus and warm gently. Season to taste.

Fill the warm vol-au-vent cases with the mixture and serve at once.

TAPENADE PASTRIES

MAKES ABOUT 30

For the pastry:
175g/6oz/1 cup plain (all-purpose) flour
pinch of salt
75g/3oz/6 tablespoons unsalted butter
2 tablespoons olive oil
iced water

For the tapenade:
12 black olives, pitted
4 anchovy fillets
1 tablespoon capers
25g/1oz/2 tablespoons canned tuna fish
½ teaspoon lemon juice
½ clove of garlic, crushed
2 tablespoons olive oil
freshly milled pepper
50g/2oz Feta cheese, crumbled
diced red pepper and dill sprigs for garnish

Sift the flour and salt into a bowl. Rub in the butter until the mixture resembles fine crumbs, then stir in the oil and sufficient water to mix to a firm dough. Cover and leave to rest in the refrigerator for at least 30 minutes.

Pureé all the ingredients for the tapenade, except the oil, in a food processor. With the machine working, pour in a slow trickle of oil until the mixture is firm but spreadable. Season with pepper.

On a lightly floured surface, roll out the pastry about 3mm/⅛ inch thick and stamp out fish (or any other decorative) shapes with a small cutter. Prick with a fork, then leave to rest in a cool place for at least 20 minutes. Bake in a preheated oven at 180°C/350°F/gas mark 4 for 15-20 minutes. Cool on a wire tray.

Spread the tapenade on each pastry shape, top with Feta cheese and garnish.

GOUGÈRES

Gougères are as familiar as an old friend and delightful with a dry white wine.

MAKES ABOUT 40

*300ml/½ pint/1¼ cups milk plus extra
for glazing
75g/3oz/6 tablespoons unsalted butter
175g/6oz/1⅓ cups plain (all-purpose)
flour, sifted
4 eggs
50g/2oz/½ cup Gruyère cheese, finely grated
50g/2oz/½ cup Cheddar cheese, finely grated
2 tablespoons freshly chopped herbs such as
parsley, chervil, dill or mint
100g/4oz/1 cup button mushrooms, diced
225g/8oz seafood such as scallops, scampi tails
and prawns (shrimp), diced
salt and freshly milled pepper*

Place the milk and 50g/2oz of the butter in a saucepan with a pinch of salt and bring to the boil. Remove from the heat, sift in the flour and beat well until a thick paste is formed. Beat in the eggs one at a time, then beat in two-thirds of each cheese and the herbs.

Heat the remaining butter and sauté the mushrooms, then add the seafood and toss very quickly. Season with salt and pepper.

Stir the seafood mixture into the cheese mixture and use to fill a piping bag fitted with a 2cm/¾ inch plain nozzle (tube). Pipe small rings about 4cm/1½ inch in diameter on to lightly buttered baking trays, brush lightly with milk and sprinkle with the remaining cheese.

Bake in a preheated oven at 200°C/400°F/gas mark 6 for 20-25 minutes until risen and golden brown. Serve warm.

ONION WEDGES

These onion wedges originate from near Lyon, the food capital of France, and typically of that area they incorporate a variety of tastes and flavours.

MAKES ABOUT 40

For the pastry:
*200g/7oz/1¾ cups plain (all-purpose)
flour, sifted
pinch of salt
100g/3½oz/7 tablespoons unsalted butter
7 teaspoons cold water*

For the filling:
*120ml/4fl oz/½ cup olive oil
500g/1lb 2oz/4 medium-sized onions,
thinly sliced
200g/7oz/¾ cup fromage frais
6 egg yolks
600ml/1 pint/2½ cups double (heavy) cream
freshly grated nutmeg
salt and freshly milled pepper
black olives, sun-dried tomatoes and parsley
leaves to garnish*

Sift the flour and salt into a bowl, then rub in the butter until the mixture resembles fine crumbs. Add the water and mix to a firm dough.

On a lightly floured surface, roll out the pastry and use to line eight 10cm/4 inch flan tins (pans). Prick the bases with a fork and chill until required.

For the filling, heat the oil and sweat the onions until translucent. Leave to cool. Beat the fromage frais, egg yolks and cream together, then stir in the onions and season with nutmeg, salt and pepper.

Transfer the mixture to the pastry cases and bake in a preheated oven at 200°F/400°F/gas mark 6 for about 25 minutes until just set.

Leave to rest for 5 minutes, then cut each flan in wedges and garnish each one with a little piece of olive, sun-dried tomato and a parsley leaf.

SALMON BURGERS

Almost anything can be made into burgers nowadays. This piquant mix of salmon tartare and smoked salmon trimmings is definitely a trendsetter.

MAKES 20

*200g/7oz salmon tartare (see page 52)
100g/4oz smoked salmon trimmings
20 buckwheat blinis (see page 46)
unsalted butter for spreading
2-3 assorted salad leaves
100ml/3½fl oz/scant ½ cup crème fraîche
1 tablespoon freshly chopped chives
sprigs of herbs such as chervil, dill or chives
to garnish*

Finely chop the salmon tartare and smoked salmon and mix together. Shape into 20 'burgers' and press firmly together.

Spread the blinis generously with butter, then place a small piece of salad leaf on each one and top with a salmon 'burger'.

Mix together the crème fraîche and chives and spoon a small amount on each burger. Garnish with sprigs of herb.

PHOTOGRAPH ON PAGE 62

TRENDY YORKSHIRE PUDDINGS

A favourite Yorkshire recipe made small. Smoked salmon, eel or trout would go just as well with the horseradish.

MAKES 30

100g/4oz/scant 1 cup plain (all-purpose) flour
2 eggs
300ml/½ pint/1¼ cups milk or milk and water
salt and freshly milled pepper
beef dripping or oil
5 tablespoons creamed horseradish
225g/8oz rare roast beef, thinly sliced
sprigs of fresh herb to garnish, such as chervil, dill

Sift the flour into a bowl, then beat in the eggs and milk to give a smooth batter. Season generously.

Place ¼ teaspoon of beef dripping or oil in each miniature muffin tin (pan) and place in a preheated oven at 220°C/425°F/gas mark 7 for a few minutes until very hot. Divide the batter between the tins and bake for about 30 minutes until well risen and crisp.

Remove the Yorkshire puddings from the tins and spoon a little creamed horseradish into each one. Shape small rosettes from the slices of beef and place one on each pudding. Dot with a little more creamed horseradish and garnish with sprigs of herbs. Serve at once.

TRENDY YORKSHIRE PUDDINGS
SALMON BURGERS
ORKNEY TURNIPS

ORKNEY TURNIPS

If you can get baby turnips with their green tops still intact then reserve them and use as lids for the filled turnips.

MAKES 30

50g/2oz/¼ cup unsalted butter
1 teaspoon caster (superfine) sugar
30 baby turnips, peeled
450g/1lb smoked finnan haddock
250ml/8fl oz/1 cup milk
8 tablespoons double (heavy) cream
½ clove of garlic, crushed
100g/4oz/1¼ cups spinach leaves, chopped
salt and freshly milled pepper

Melt half the butter in a saucepan. Add the sugar and turnips and toss well over a medium heat to glaze them. Just cover with water and season with salt and pepper. Cover and simmer until just tender. Cut the tops from the turnips and carefully scoop out the centres to make small containers. Remove the skin and bones from the smoked haddock and poach in the milk until the fish flakes easily. Drain, reserving the milk.

Reduce the milk by fast boiling, then add the cream and reduce again to give a thick consistency. Chop the fish and add to the sauce.

Sweat the garlic in the remaining butter, then add the spinach and toss quickly until just wilted. Drain on a kitchen cloth (dish towel).

Place a little spinach in each turnip and top with the smoked haddock mixture. Serve at once.

WELSH PASTRIES

A twist of the traditional Welsh leek ideal for patriots on St David's Day.

MAKES ABOUT 40

For the pastry:
150g/5oz/1¼ cups plain (all-purpose) flour
pinch of salt
75g/3oz/6 tablespoons unsalted butter
1 tablespoon freshly chopped tarragon
1 egg yolk
4 teaspoons cold water

For the filling:
15g/½oz/1 tablespoon unsalted butter
1 tablespoon finely chopped onion
1 small clove of garlic, crushed
75g/3oz/½ cup leek, cut in tiny squares
25g/1oz/¼ cup pine kernels
1 egg
200ml/7fl oz/scant 1 cup double (heavy) cream
salt and freshly milled pepper
50g/2oz/½ cup Emmenthal cheese, finely grated

For the pastry, sift the flour and salt into a bowl and rub in the butter until the mixture resembles fine crumbs. Stir in the tarragon, then add the egg yolk and water and work to a firm, manageable dough.

On a lightly floured surface, roll out the pastry and use to line about 40 miniature (about 1 tablespoon capacity) tartlet tins (pans). Place on a baking tray and chill until required.

For the filling, melt the butter and sweat the onion and garlic until translucent. Add the leek and sweat until tender. Leave to cool, then stir in the pine kernels and season with salt and pepper. Beat the egg and cream together and stir in the leek mixture.

Fill the pastry cases with the mixture and sprinkle each one with a little cheese. Bake in a preheated oven at 220°C/425°F/gas mark 7 for 10 minutes until set and golden.

Leave to cool for a few minutes, then unmould from the tins. Serve warm.

ESCARGOTS EN ROBE

What could be more French than garlic snails, mushrooms, wine and a racy recipe proven over hundreds of years?

MAKES 40

15g/½oz/1 tablespoon unsalted butter
1 shallot, finely chopped
1 clove of garlic, crushed
75g/3oz/¾ cup mushrooms, finely chopped
120ml/4fl oz/½ cup dry white wine
120ml/4fl oz/½ cup veal or chicken stock
250ml/8fl oz/1 cup double (heavy) cream
salt and freshly milled pepper
40 snails from a can, drained
40 small vol-au-vent cases, freshly baked
freshly chopped parsley to garnish

Heat the butter and sweat the shallot and garlic until translucent. Add the mushrooms, wine and stock and reduce by half by fast boiling.

Stir in the cream and reduce again to give about 200ml/7fl oz/scant 1 cup sauce. Season to taste. Stir in the snails and warm gently.

Spoon a snail and a little sauce into each vol-au-vent case and sprinkle with a little chopped parsley. Serve warm.

TEMPURA FISH WITH VEGETABLES

The secret of tempura is the lightness of the batter and the fact that it should be eaten very quickly after it has been fried. Instead of using fish fillets, try whitebait. Always serve with Japanese pickled ginger and crisp spring onion strips.

400g/14oz fish fillets such as salmon, monkfish, cod, haddock or sole, skinned
300ml/½ pint/1¼ cups vegetable oil
120ml/4fl oz/½ cup sesame oil
50g/2oz/⅓ cup kohlrabi, cut in sticks
50g/2oz/½ cup carrot, cut in sticks
50g/2oz/1 cup small broccoli or cauliflower florets
50g/2oz/⅓ cup button onions, sliced
soy sauce
Japanese pickled ginger
spring onions (scallions) cut in julienne strips

For the batter:
2 eggs
120ml/4fl oz/½ cup iced water
generous pinch (⅛ teaspoon) of bicarbonate of soda (baking soda)
65g/2½oz/7 tablespoons plain (all-purpose) flour

Cut the fish fillets in small strips and dry on an absorbent cloth.

For the batter, whisk the eggs and water until pale and foamy. Add the bicarbonate of soda and flour and mix in quickly.

Heat the two oils together to 200°C/400°F on a sugar thermometer. Dip the fish and vegetables into the batter and drop into the hot oil in batches. Fry until crisp and golden, then drain on absorbent paper and serve at once with soy sauce, pickled ginger and spring onions.

SCAMPI IN A CRUST

In its preparation this dish is, to say the least, old-fashioned. Using some of the finest British produce, it has been with us for centuries.

A warming, easy to eat little canapé – perhaps served by an open fire with a shot of single malt whisky to round it of.

MAKES 30

200ml/7fl oz/scant 1 cup double (heavy) cream
75g/3oz/²⁄₃ cup crab meat
50g/2oz/¹⁄₃ cup lobster, finely chopped
1 tablespoon Béchamel sauce (see page 137)
1 teaspoon freshly chopped mint
salt and freshly milled pepper
30 raw langoustine tails or raw prawns (shrimp), shelled and de-veined
plain flour
beaten egg
fresh white breadcrumbs
oil for deep frying

Reduce the cream by fast boiling to a very thick mixture. Stir in the crab meat, lobster, Béchamel sauce and mint. Season to taste. Continue cooking until very thick once more. Leave to go cold.

Split the langoustine tails or prawns in half, taking care that they are still attached at the top and tail ends to make each one into a ring. Fill the centre of each 'ring' with a little filling. Season with salt and pepper, then dip in plain flour, beaten egg and finally breadcrumbs until evenly coated. Repeat the egg and crumb layers once more.

Heat the oil and fry the prepared langoustine tails in batches until crisp and golden. Drain on absorbent paper. Serve warm.

CHEESE PALMIERS WITH AUBERGINE (EGGPLANT)

MAKES 40

250g/9oz puff pastry
beaten egg to white to glaze
40g/1¹⁄₂oz/¹⁄₃ cup Parmesan cheese, grated
1 medium-sized aubergine (eggplant), cut in small dice
salt and freshly milled pepper
50ml/2fl oz/¹⁄₄ cup olive oil
50g/2oz/¹⁄₃ cup onion, finely chopped
1 clove of garlic, crushed
100g/4oz/6 tablespoons tomato fillets, diced
50g/2oz/¹⁄₃ cup pine kernels, roasted
2 tablespoons freshly chopped coriander (cilantro)
40 coriander (cilantro) leaves to garnish

On a lightly floured surface, roll out the pastry to a rectangle measuring 28 × 18cm/11 × 7 inches.

Brush the pastry with egg white and sprinkle with about half the cheese. Fold the long edges in to meet in the centre. Brush the pastry with egg white and sprinkle with half the remaining cheese. Fold the pastry in half along its length.

Chill the pastry for about 20 minutes, then cut in 40 thin slices. Place them on a lightly buttered baking tray and sprinkle with the remaining cheese. Press gently to flatten each piece of pastry slightly.

Bake in a preheated oven at 220°C/425°F/gas mark 7 for 10 minutes, then turn the palmiers over and bake for a further 5 minutes until crisp and golden. Cool on a wire tray.

Sprinkle the aubergine with salt and leave for 15 minutes to remove the bitter juices. Wash thoroughly.

Heat the oil in a saucepan and sweat the onion until translucent, then add the garlic and cook for a further 1 minute. Stir in the aubergine and tomato, cover and simmer for about 10 minutes until the aubergine is tender. Stir in the pine kernels and chopped coriander and re-duce any remaining liquid by fast boiling. Season to taste.

Spoon a little aubergine mixture on to each palmier and garnish with a coriander leaf.

MATJES MOUTHFULS

MAKES 20

5 matjes herring fillets
5 tablespoons soured cream
¹⁄₄ dessert apple, thinly sliced
20g/³⁄₄oz/2¹⁄₂ tablespoons onion, finely chopped
2 teaspoons chopped chives
5 slices of rye bread or pumpernickel
unsalted butter for spreading
20 small lettuce leaves
40g/1¹⁄₂oz/¹⁄₃ cup cooked beetroot (beets), sliced

Soak the matjes herring fillets for at least 1 hour in cold water or milk to remove some of the salt. Wash under cold run-ning water, dry on a kitchen cloth (dish towels) and cut each fillet in four pieces.

Mix the soured cream, apple, onion and half the chives.

Spread the bread with butter and cut in triangles. Place a small lettuce leaf and a slice of beetroot on each piece of bread. Top with a piece of herring fillet and a spoonful of the soured cream mixture. Sprinkle with the remaining chives.

PETITES PIZZAS

Individual pizzas are perfect for a lunchtime party especially for the young. Choose from three different toppings.

MAKES ABOUT 10

For the dough:
15g/¹/2oz/1 cake fresh yeast
1 teaspoon caster (superfine) sugar
100ml/3¹/2fl oz/scant ¹/2 cup warm water
225g/8oz/scant 2 cups strong (bread) plain flour
salt
50ml/2fl oz/¹/4 cup vegetable or olive oil

Mix the yeast and sugar with a little of the water and leave for 5 minutes in a warm place.

Sift the flour and a large pinch of salt into a bowl and mix in the yeast, oil and remaining water to a firm dough. Knead for about 5 minutes. Cover and leave to prove in a warm place until doubled in size.

Knead the dough once more, then divide in 10-12 pieces. On a lightly floured surface roll out the small pieces of dough to rounds about 7.5cm/3 inch in diameter, leaving them slightly thicker around the edges. Then follow the directions given for the chosen topping.

PETITES PIZZAS

TOPPINGS

SPINACH WITH EMMENTHAL AND ANCHOVIES

1 clove of garlic, crushed
1 tablespoon olive oil plus extra for brushing
200g/7oz/scant 1 cup spinach purée
40g/1¹/2oz/6-8 anchovy fillets, quartered
100g/4oz Emmenthal cheese, sliced
100g/4oz Emmenthal cheese, sliced
50ml/2fl oz/¹/4 cup milk
salt and freshly milled pepper

Sweat the garlic in the oil until nutty, then add the spinach. Season to taste.

Brush the pizza bases with a little oil, place on an oiled baking tray and spread with spinach. Arrange pieces of anchovy on top. Dip the slices of Emmenthal in the milk and arrange on top of the pizzas.

Bake in a preheated oven at 220°C/425°F/gas mark 7 for 8-10 minutes. Serve warm.

PESTO WITH TOMATOES AND WILD MUSHROOMS

15g/¹/2oz/1¹/2 tablespoons shallot, finely chopped
2 tablespoons olive oil plus extra for brushing
1 small clove of garlic, crushed
175g/6oz/1¹/2 cups wild mushrooms, sliced
4 plum tomatoes, thinly sliced
4 tablespoons pesto (see page 135)
4 tablespoons grated Parmesan cheese
salt and freshly milled pepper

Sweat the shallot in the olive oil until translucent, then add the garlic and wild mushrooms. Season with salt and pep-per. Cook quickly until any liquid has evaporated.

Brush the pizza bases with a little olive oil and place on an oiled baking tray. Arrange the tomato slices on each one and top with the mushroom mixture. Dot with pesto and sprinkle with the Parmesan cheese. Bake in a preheated oven at 220°C/425°F/gas mark 7 for 8-10 minutes. Serve warm.

TOMATO, CHILLI AND GOAT'S CHEESE

40g/1¹/2oz/¹/4 cup spring onion (scallion), finely chopped
100ml/3¹/2fl oz/scant ¹/2 cup olive oil
2 tomatoes, thinly sliced – use red and yellow if available
2 teaspoons fresh rosemary sprigs
1 red chilli, seeded and finely chopped
1 green chilli, seeded and finely chopped
4 Crottin Chauvignolles cheeses, thinly sliced
salt and freshly milled pepper

Sweat the spring onion in a little of the oil, then add the tomatoes. Season with salt and pepper.

Mix the rosemary and chillies with the remaining oil and pour over the thinly sliced cheese. Leave to marinate for about 20 minutes.

Arrange some tomato mixture on each pizza base, then place on an oiled baking tray. Top with the cheese adding the rosemary and chillies. Bake in a preheated oven at 220°C/425°F/gas mark 7 for 8-10 minutes. Serve warm.

BRIOCHE SOUFFLÉS

Here is something for the daring cook. Like all soufflés, if you use the right technique and follow the stages of preparation carefully it really isn't any problem at all. Too much is made of the difficulties of a soufflé, so follow the recipe carefully and impress your guests by suggesting that it's child's play to make a good soufflé!

MAKES ABOUT 40

For the brioches:
25g/1oz/1½ cakes fresh yeast
1 teaspoon malt extract
25g/1oz/2 tablespoons caster (superfine) sugar
25ml/1fl oz/2 tablespoons warm milk
250g/9oz/heaped 2 cups strong (bread)
plain flour
100ml/3½fl oz beaten egg (2-3)
1 teaspoon salt
75g/3oz/6 tablespoons unsalted butter

For the filling:
40g/1½oz/3 tablespoons unsalted butter
75g/3oz/½ cup shallot, finely chopped
175g/6oz/1½ cups wild mushrooms,
finely chopped

For the soufflé topping:
50g/2oz/¼ cup unsalted butter
50g/2oz/5 tablespoons plain (all-purpose) flour
300ml/½ pint/1¼ cups milk
4 eggs, separated
3 egg whites
salt and freshly milled pepper

Mix the yeast with the malt extract, sugar and milk. Sift the flour into a bowl and add the yeast mixture, beaten egg and salt. Beat well to form a dough, then cover and leave to rise in a warm place until doubled in size. Beat in the butter until smooth, then cover the dough and leave in a cool place to rest for 6-8 hours.

Knead the dough lightly, then break off small pieces weighing about 15g/½oz and shape into small balls. Place in buttered miniature brioche tins (pans) and leave in a warm place to prove until doubled in size.

Bake in a preheated oven at 230°C/450°F/gas mark 8 for about 10 minutes until risen and golden. Cool on a wire tray.

For the filling, melt the butter in a saucepan and sweat the shallot and mushrooms until the shallot is translucent and the liquid has been absorbed. Season generously.

For the soufflé topping, melt the butter in a saucepan, then stir in the flour and cook, stirring, for 1-2 minutes to make a roux.

Heat the milk and gradually stir into the roux until smooth. Beat in the egg yolks and season generously. Whisk the egg whites until stiff and fold into the mixture until evenly combined.

Cut off the tops of the brioches and hollow out the centres to form little cups. Spoon a little mushroom mixture into each one and top with some soufflé mixture.

Bake in a preheated oven at 230°C/450°F/gas mark 8 for 4-5 minutes until risen and golden. Serve at once.

ROSTI WITH SMOKED EEL

Central European cultures are far more appreciative of the eel, but we are producing a far better quality of smoked eel in this country than ever before.

MAKES 20

450g/1lb potatoes
1 tablespoon freshly chopped rosemary
pinch of nutmeg
salt and freshly milled white pepper
25g/1oz/2 tablespoons unsalted butter
50ml/2fl oz/¼ cup olive oil
4 tablespoons double (heavy) cream
2 teaspoons freshly grated horseradish
½ teaspoon white wine vinegar or lemon juice
1 tablespoon freshly chopped chives
100g/4oz smoked eel fillet
5 radishes, cut in fine julienne

Peel and coarsely grate the potatoes, then place in a clean kitchen cloth (dish towel) and squeeze out all the water.

Mix the potatoes with the rosemary, nutmeg, salt and pepper. Divide the mixture into 20 even-sized portions.

Heat half the butter and oil in a large frying pan and place ten portions of potato in the pan. Press each one firmly to compress it and fry for about 10 minutes, turning occasionally until crisp and golden on both sides. Keep warm. Heat the remaining butter and oil and fry the remaining potato mixture.

Lightly whip the cream, then fold in the horseradish, vinegar or lemon juice and chives. Top each potato rosti with a small amount of horseradish cream, a little smoked eel fillet and some radish julienne.

BRIE TARTLETS

You could learn to like this little French canapé more than yourself! It must be eaten warm from the grill.

MAKES ABOUT 30

For the pastry:
100g/4oz/½ cup unsalted butter
225g/8oz/scant 2 cups plain (all-purpose)
flour, sieved
pinch of salt
8 teaspoons cold water

For the filling:
175g/6oz Brie cheese, rind removed
2 egg yolks
175ml/6fl oz/¾ cup single (thin) cream
pinch of nutmeg
salt and freshly milled pepper

For the garnish:
cranberry sauce (optional)
sprigs of dill or flat leaf parsley

Rub the butter into the flour and salt, then mix to a firm dough with the water. Leave to rest in a cool place for 20 minutes, then roll out and use to line miniature muffin tins (pans). Bake blind in a preheated oven at 200°C/400°F/gas mark 6 for 15-20 minutes.

Combine all the ingredients for the filling in a food processor and work until smooth.

Remove the pastry cases from the tins and arrange on a baking tray. Fill the cases with the Brie cheese mixture and place under a preheated grill until lightly set and golden.

Allow to cool slightly, then top each tartlet with a little cranberry sauce, if wished, and a sprig of herb.

GAME AND CHESTNUT CHIPOLATAS

A late autumn or winter canapé with the delight of chestnuts back in season and the rich flavour of game.

MAKES ABOUT 30

200g/7oz lean venison (or any other game)
50g/2oz/¼ cup unsalted butter
2 tablespoons finely chopped onion
1 egg white
200ml/7fl oz/scant 1 cup double (heavy) cream
6 cooked chestnuts, chopped
2 teaspoons freshly chopped marjoram or thyme
salt and freshly milled pepper
75g/3oz/6 tablespoons chestnut purée
about 30 bilberries (blueberries) or redcurrants
about 30 tiny sprigs of mint

Dice the venison, discarding any sinew.

Melt 15g/½oz/1 tablespoon of the butter and sauté the onion until translucent. Combine the onion and venison and mince (grind) finely or work in a food processor until fairly smooth.

Place the mixture in a bowl set over ice and slowly beat in the egg white and then the cream. Add the chestnuts and herbs and season generously. (Cook and taste a small amount to check the seasoning and adjust as necessary.)

Using a piping bag fitted with 2cm/¾ inch nozzle (tube), pipe 15-18cm/6-7 inch lengths of mixture on to pieces of cling film, or pipe into sausage skins, if available. Wrap the cling film around each length of the mixture twisting the ends of each stip to make 'sausages'. Tie the sausage skin at 15-18cm/6-7 inch intervals with string. Poach in simmer-ing water – it must not boil – for 10 minutes, then drain and refresh in iced water. Remove the sausages from their wrappings.

Melt the remaining butter in a frying pan and slowly fry the sausages until lightly browned on all sides. Remove from the pan and cool slightly. Cut the sausages in 2.5-4cm/1-1½ inch lengths. Using a piping bag fitted with a small star nozzle, pipe a rosette of chestnut purée on each piece and top with a bilberry or redcurrant and a sprig of mint.

QUAILS' EGG KOFTAS WITH PROVENÇALE SAUCE

H O T

A N D

Spicy

If you think of hot and spicy food, you think of the Far East, India, Malaysia, Korea and Thailand, but nearer to home there are the Arab influences of Morocco, Tunisia, Egypt and Turkey which offer endless ideas.

The cooking of Bangkok has probably had the greatest influence on me. Spices and herbs are used in great harmony. In spite of the fact that there are a large variety and number in almost all Thai dishes, the flavours are brought together very cleverly, almost scientifically, without degrading the main ingredient, be it vegetable or fish, shellfish or meat. Artistic flair and expertise in the presentation and serving of food, as well as the very important place food holds in a society such as this, adds up to a fascinating insight into its culture.

EXCEPTION

A new cocktail created for us by
Peter Dorelli, Head Barman at
The Savoy.

½ tequila
¼ cointreau
¼ lime juice
2 dashes of Calvados
2 dashes of framboise

Shake with ice.

QUAILS' EGG KOFTAS

The Chef of the Taj Mahal hotel in Bombay inspired these spicy morsels, although they are also reminiscent of the good old British scotch egg. Surprisingly, tomato ketchup also makes a very good dipping sauce to go with them.

MAKES 20

50g/2oz/¼ cup red lentils
8 green cardamom pods
1 teaspoon cumin seeds
1 dried red chilli
1 teaspoon whole cloves
4 black peppercorns
2.5cm/1 inch piece of cinnamon stick
225g/8oz/1 cup minced (ground) lamb
25g/1oz/3 tablespoons onion, chopped
2 cloves of garlic, chopped
¼ teaspoon salt
450ml/¾ pint/scant 2 cups water
2 tablespoons freshly chopped mint
2 tablespoons freshly chopped parsley
1 egg yolk
20 quails' eggs
oil for deep frying
Provençale sauce to serve (see page 133)

Soak the lentils in cold water for 10 minutes, then drain.

Remove the black seeds from the cardamom pods and combine with the other spices. Grind to a fine powder in a coffee mill.

Place the lentils, spices, lamb, onion, garlic, salt and water in a saucepan and bring to the boil. Reduce the heat, cover and simmer for 20 minutes. Remove the lid and cook over a medium heat for another 20 minutes, stirring occasionally until the meat is completely dry and the liquid has been absorbed.

Place the mixture in a food processor with the mint, parsley and egg yolk and work to a smooth paste. (It is essential that it really is a smooth paste so that it can be easily shaped.) Leave to cool.

Cook the quails' eggs in boiling salted water for 3 minutes. Drain and refresh in iced water, then carefully peel away the shell. Wrap a small amount of the lamb mixture around each egg to completely encase it, pressing it firmly in place.

Heat the oil and deep fry the koftas until crisp and golden. Drain on absorbent paper. If wished, cut in half. Serve warm or cold with Provençale sauce handed separately.

PHOTOGRAPH ON PAGE 70

MUSHROOM AND CUCUMBER MORSELS

This particularly oriental-flavoured dish is a nice addition to most cocktail parties.

MAKES ABOUT 30

75g/3oz/6 tablespoons unsalted butter
1 large red (sweet) pepper, skinned and finely diced
1 medium-sized apple, peeled and finely diced
100g/4oz/¾ cup onion, finely diced
1 clove garlic, crushed
1 teaspoon medium-hot curry powder
pinch of saffron threads
120ml/4fl oz/½ cup vegetable stock
50ml/2fl oz/¼ cup double (heavy) cream, whipped
salt and freshly milled pepper
30 button mushrooms
about ¾ of a cucumber

Melt half the butter in a saucepan and sweat the red pepper, apple, onion and garlic until soft. Add the curry powder and saffron and cook for 1-2 minutes. Then add the stock and boil for 3 minutes. Cool and liquidise (blend). Fold in the whipped cream and season to taste.

Trim the mushrooms. Cut the cucumber in quarters lengthways and discard the seeds. Cut the cucumber in short lengths and using a turning knife, shape in small barrel shapes about the same size as the mushrooms.

Melt the remaining butter in a frying pan and sauté the mushrooms. Add the cucumber and warm through.

Thread a mushroom and piece of cucumber on each cocktail stick (toothpick). Arrange in a dish with the sauce poured over or hand the sauce separately.

MEXICAN CLAM SHELLS

Clams are relatively little used in this country, whilst in North America, the Far East, Italy and Portugal they are considered to be a delicacy. Perhaps this spicy mouthful will give you the same idea!

MAKES 40

40 small cherrystone clams
200ml/7fl oz/scant 1¼ cups dry white wine
65g/2½oz/1 cup young spinach leaves, blanched
1 tablespoon olive oil
2 red chillies, seeds removed and finely chopped
250ml/8fl oz/1 cup Provençale sauce (see page 133)
2 teaspoons freshly chopped chives

Wash the clams well under cold running water. Ensure that they are all firmly shut. Place the clams in a saucepan and add the white wine. Cover with a lid and cook over a high heat for 3-5 minutes, shaking frequently until the shells are all open. Remove the clams from their shells and reserve one half of each shell.

Thoroughly drain the spinach and chop finely. Divide between the clam shells.

Heat the oil and sweat the chillies, then add the Provençale sauce and cook for about 5 minutes until thickened. Stir in the clams to reheat, then spoon a little of the mixture into each shell. Sprinkle with chopped chives. Serve warm.

MADRAS MUSSELS

Mussels with garlic, and mussels with mushrooms are both great combinations but mussels with a hint of curry is the best combination, especially with a tiny amount of flaked almond on the top to give a hint of sweetness.

MAKES 20

20 very fresh large mussels
100g/4oz/²⁄₃ cup combined onion, leek and celery, diced
1 small clove of garlic
250ml/8fl oz/1 cup dry white wine
about 85ml/3fl oz/⅓ cup curry sauce (see page 136)
flaked almonds, toasted, to sprinkle
shredded fresh chillies (optional)
sea salt to serve

Scrub the mussels well under cold running water. Discard the beards.

Place the mussels in a large saucepan with the vegetables, garlic and wine. Cover and cook over a high heat for about 3 minutes until the mussels are open. Discard any which remain closed. Strain the mussels. (The stock may be kept and frozen for a soup or sauce.)

Loosen each mussel, then replace it in a half shell. Warm the curry sauce and spoon a little over each mussel. Sprinkle with flaked almonds and shredded fresh chillies. Serve on a bed of sea salt with cocktail sticks (toothpicks) at the side.

MADRAS MUSSELS
SPICED NUTS
MEXICAN CLAM SHELLS

SPICED NUTS

Who can resist a nut – in texture and flavour quite different from other foods served at a party?

MAKES 225g/8oz/2 CUPS

15g/¹/₂oz/1 tablespoon unsalted butter
1 tablespoon vegetable oil
225g/8oz/2 cups assorted blanched nuts such as
almonds, hazelnuts, cashew nuts and
Brazil nuts
2 teaspoons medium-hot curry powder
1 teaspoon sea salt

Heat the butter and oil in a roasting tin (pan). Add the nuts, curry powder and salt and toss well until evenly mixed.

Roast the nuts in a preheated oven at 190°C/375°F/gas mark 5 for about 20 minutes, turning occasionally until golden.

Leave to cool, then toss well. Serve at once or store in an airtight container.

PHOTOGRAPH ON PAGE 75

TURKISH MOONS

These little puff pastries are similar to snacks found on street stalls in Istanbul.

MAKES ABOUT 50

25g/1oz/2 tablespoons unsalted butter
100g/4oz/³/₄ cup onion, finely chopped
450g/1lb/2 cups minced (ground) lamb
¹/₂ teaspoon ground allspice
¹/₄ teaspoon chilli powder
50g/2oz/¹/₃ cup dried apricots, finely chopped
25g/1oz/3 tablespoons shelled walnuts or
pistachios, chopped
2 tomatoes, skinned and chopped
2 tablespoons freshly chopped parsley
1 teaspoon salt
450g/1lb puff pastry
beaten egg to glaze

Melt the butter and sweat the onion until transparent. Add the minced lamb and spices and cook over a medium heat until the meat is well browned. Add the apricots, walnuts and tomatoes and cook until the liquid has been absorbed. Add the parsley and season with the salt. Leave to cool.

On a lightly floured surface, roll out the pastry thinly and stamp out about 50 7.5cm/3 inch rounds, using the trimmings as necessary. Brush with beaten egg and place a little of the filling in the centre of each one. Fold each one over and press the edges to seal well. Brush with beaten egg. Leave to rest in a cool place for at least 20 minutes.

Place on a lightly greased baking tray and bake in a preheated oven at 220°C/425°F/gas mark 7 for 12-15 minutes until crisp and golden brown. Serve warm.

BASQUE POTATOES

Potatoes are very often undervalued as a cocktail food. This potato dish is one of many which originate in Spain.

MAKES ABOUT 20

2 tablespoons olive oil
2 tablespoons finely chopped onion or shallot
1 teaspoon paprika
1 teaspoon cumin seeds
¹/₄ teaspoon cayenne
450g/1lb small even-sized new
potatoes, scrubbed
300ml/¹/₂ pint/1¹/₄ cups tomato juice or passata
300ml/¹/₂ pint/1¹/₄ cups water
salt
freshly chopped parsley to garnish

Heat the oil in a wide shallow saucepan and sweat the onion and spices until the onion is translucent.

Add the potatoes and toss well in the spices. Add the tomato juice or passata and water and bring to the boil. Add a little salt and simmer gently, uncovered, for 20-25 minutes until the potatoes are tender and the liquid reduced to a thick coating sauce.

Season to taste with salt, then sprinkle with chopped parsley and spike each potato with a cocktail stick (toothpick). Serve warm.

CHILLI CROÛTONS

This canapé is ideal served with beer, cider or best of all Grappa.

MAKES 20

20g/³⁄4oz/1½ tablespoons unsalted butter
75g/3oz/²⁄3 cup button mushrooms, sliced
1 small red chilli, seeds removed and finely chopped
1 small green chilli, seeds removed and finely chopped
50g/2oz/¼ cup Parma ham (prosciutto) trimmings, diced
5 slices of rye or multi-grain bread, toasted
2 tablespoons freshly chopped parsley
1 tablespoon freshly chopped oregano
50g/2oz/scant ½ cup Parmesan cheese, grated

Melt the butter and sauté the mushrooms until golden. Combine with the chillies and ham.

Trim the crusts off the bread and cut each slice in quarters. Arrange a little mushroom filling on each piece and sprinkle with half the herbs. Mix the remaining herbs with the Parmesan cheese and sprinkle on top.

Place under a preheated grill (broiler) and brown quickly.

THAI CURRY BITES

Quite a number of the frivolities in this book include ideas brought back from a working holiday at the Oriental Hotel in Bangkok. Of course, there is the heat of Indian curries which can be quite fiery but not elegant; Chinese food is more refined and Japanese food beautifully presented, but Thai food combines elegance with spiciness. The Savoy now produces some beautiful Thai canapés.

The lemon grass, chillies, garlic, ginger and coriander bring intense tastes and flavours which are explosive, but can be controlled by the addition of coconut milks and creams when necessary.

It is very important that none of the food is cooked for too long.

MAKES 30

450g/1lb skinless and boneless chicken breasts
75g/3oz/6 tablespoons unsalted butter
40g/1½oz/2½ tablespoon fresh root ginger, peeled and finely chopped
2 cloves of garlic, crushed
¼ teaspoon green peppercorns
1 stalk of lemon grass, finely chopped
2 red chillies, finely chopped
1 teaspoon fish stock or chicken stock
2 teaspoons lime juice
½ teaspoon ground coriander
400ml/14fl oz/1¾ cups coconut milk
2 teaspoons freshly chopped coriander (cilantro) leaves
salt and freshly milled pepper

Cut the chicken in 30 even-sized pieces. Heat 50g/2oz/¼ cup of the butter in a large frying pan and sauté the chicken pieces until lightly browned on all sides.

Melt the remaining butter in the same frying pan and sauté the ginger, garlic, peppercorns, lemon grass and chillies. Add the fish stock, lime juice and ground coriander. Gradually stir in the coconut milk, bring to the boil, then reduce the heat and simmer for 8-10 minutes. Cool slightly, then purée in a liquidiser (blender) and pass through a fine sieve. Warm the sauce gently, stir in the coriander leaves and season to taste.

Place cocktail sticks (toothpicks) in the pieces of chicken and arrange on a serving dish. Spoon the sauce over the chicken or serve separately as a dipping sauce.

The chicken pieces may be reheated in the sauce.

PHOTOGRAPH ON PAGE 82

SESAME TOASTS

A popular party food amongst adults and children alike.

If using frozen prawns (shrimp), make sure that you have 150g/5oz weight when defrosted and excess moisture has been squeezed out of the prawns. This may mean thawing up to 300g/10oz.

MAKES 20

150g/5oz peeled cooked prawns (shrimp) or
preferably raw prawns, well drained
1 large egg white
1 teaspoon cornflour (cornstarch)
1 teaspoon lemon juice
½ teaspoon light soy sauce
½ small clove of garlic, crushed
1 teaspoon Dijon mustard
1.5cm/½ inch piece of root ginger, chopped
5 slices of white bread, crusts removed
3 tablespoons sesame seeds
oil for deep frying

Place the prawns (shrimp), egg white, cornflour, lemon juice, soy sauce, garlic and mustard in a food processor. Place the ginger in a garlic press and squeeze the juice over the ingredients in the food processor. Work to a paste.

Spread the prawn (shrimp) paste evenly over the slices of bread and press the sesame seeds on top. Cut each slice in four triangles.

Heat the oil and fry the slices until the bread is crisp and golden. Drain on absorbent paper. Serve at once.

Any number of other shapes may be stamped out.

MARINATED CHICKEN ALANYA

Alanya, a very charming little town on the Aegean Coast, inspired this delightful and refreshing chicken dish with its yoghurt and cucumber sauce.

MAKES ABOUT 30

400g/14oz/2 cups skinless and boneless
chicken breast
50ml/2fl oz/¼ cup soy sauce
250ml/8fl oz/1 cup natural yoghurt
1 clove of garlic, skinned and crushed
100g/4oz/½ cup cucumber, peeled, seeds
removed and finely diced
salt and freshly milled pepper
oil for deep frying
mint sprigs to garnish

Cut the chicken in small pieces and place in a bowl. Add the soy sauce and about one-third of the yoghurt and mix well. Cover and leave in the refrigerator for about 12 hours, then drain thoroughly. Combine the remaining yoghurt with the garlic and cucumber to make a dip. Season to taste.

Heat the oil and deep fry the well-drained chicken pieces until crisp and golden. Drain on absorbent paper and serve at once with the dip. Garnish with sprigs of mint.

FRITTO MISTO IN CHILLI BATTER

This should be fried and served immediately whilst still very hot. It goes well with good white wine or Champagne as the spicing of the seafood is delicate.

SERVES 8

100g/4oz fillet of sole, skinned
100g/4oz fillet of salmon, skinned
100g/4oz scallops
100g/4oz raw scampi tails
100g/4oz squid, cut in rings
salt and freshly milled pepper
125g/4½oz/heaped 1 cup plain
(all-purpose) flour
150ml/¼ pint/¾ cup lager or light ale
1 egg white
1 red chilli, seeds removed and finely chopped
1 green chilli, seeds removed and finely chopped
oil for deep frying

Cut the sole and salmon in strips about 1cm/⅜ inch thick. Cut the scallops in slices about 5mm/¼ inch thick. Season all the pieces of fish, then toss them in 20g/¾oz/2 tablespoons of the measured flour and keep to one side.

Mix the remaining flour with the lager or light ale until smooth. Whisk the egg white with a pinch of salt until stiff, then fold into the batter with the chopped chillies.

Dip the pieces of fish into the batter and deep fry in batches until crisp and golden. Drain on an absorbent cloth. Serve at once.

ANCHOVY SURPRISE

Be careful to use good quality anchovy as the cheap variety is often very salty and can spoil the combination and balance of this most unusual dish. Offal is generally undervalued, so people who do not normally use it may be interested to try this completely different taste.

MAKES 30

2 veal brains
50g/2oz/3½ tablespoons combined leek, carrot and celery, diced
1 onion, skinned
2 whole cloves
1 bay leaf
40g/1½oz/6 – 8 anchovy fillets, puréed
plain (all-purpose) flour
1 tablespoon vegetable oil
15g/½oz/1 tablespoon unsalted butter
½ ripe avocado
50ml/2fl oz/¼ cup chicken stock
salt and freshly milled white pepper
30 thin slices cut from a French stick
100g/4oz/½ cup garlic butter (see page 137)
freshly chopped parsley to garnish

Soak the brains in cold water for 1 hour, then rinse under cold running water until the blood is removed. Carefully discard any membrane.

Place in a saucepan with the diced vegetables, and the onion studded with the cloves and bay leaf. Cover with cold water and bring to the boil. Simmer for 25 minutes. Drain and cool.

Spread the anchovy purée over the surface of the brains, then dust lightly with flour. Heat the oil and butter and sauté the brains until golden brown on all sides.

Purée the avocado with the chicken stock and season to taste with salt and pepper.

Spread the bread slices with garlic butter and toast until crisp and golden brown on both sides. Spread with a little avocado purée. Cut the brains in thin slices and place one on each piece of toast. Sprinkle with chopped parsley and serve at once.

CHORIZO MUSHROOMS

The combination of strongly flavoured Spanish chorizo sausage and the mildness of mushrooms make these an ideal little bite to serve on their own before lunch or dinner with a dry sherry tapas-style.

MAKES 30

30 medium-sized cap mushrooms weighing about 15g/½oz each
olive oil
225g/8oz chorizo sausage

Wipe the mushrooms and discard the stalks. Brush each mushroom cap with a little olive oil and place on a baking tray.

Cut the sausage in small pieces and fit one inside each mushroom cap to replace the stalk. Bake in a preheated oven at 220°C/425°F/gas mark 7 for 10 minutes. Brush the mushrooms again with the oil on the tray. Serve warm.

CHINESE SPARE RIBS

Chinese five-spice powder combined with the other flavouring ingredients gives these spare ribs a unique scent and flavour.

MAKES ABOUT 30

900g/2lb pork spare ribs, cut in 5-7.5cm/2-3 inch pieces
1 tablespoon yellow bean paste
2 tablespoons soy sauce
1cm/½ inch piece of root ginger, grated
2 cloves of garlic, crushed
2 teaspoons Chinese five-spice powder
2 tablespoons sherry or rice wine

Place the spare ribs in a roasting tin (pan).

Combine all the remaining ingredients and add to the ribs. Toss well to coat evenly, then leave to marinate for at least 8 hours in a cool place.

Roast in a preheated oven at 190°C/375°F/gas mark 5 for about 1 hour until crisp and tender, turning from time to time and draining off excess fat. Serve at once.

DEEP FRIED CRAB CLAWS

MAKES 20

20 shelled crab claws
juice of 1 lime
1 teaspoon Worcestershire sauce
1 teaspoon Tabasco sauce
salt and freshly milled pepper
25g/1oz/2½ tablespoons plain (all-purpose)
flour
1-2 eggs, beaten
50g/2oz/1 cup fresh white breadcrumbs
oil for deep frying
rémoulade sauce (see page 136) to serve

Marinate the crab claws in lime juice, Worcestershire sauce and Tabasco for at least 1 hour or up to 24 hours. Drain and season with salt and pepper.

Dip the crab claws in flour, then in beaten egg and breadcrumbs until evenly coated. Deep fry in hot oil until crisp and golden. Drain on absorbent kitchen paper.

Serve at once with rémoulade sauce handed separately.

VEAL BITKIS

MAKES 20

2 tablespoons vegetable oil
75g/3oz/½ cup onion, finely chopped
1 clove of garlic, crushed
400g/14oz lean veal or other white
meat trimmings
1 egg
120ml/4fl oz/½ cup double (heavy) cream
½ teaspoon white peppercorns, crushed
120ml/4fl oz/½cup dry white wine
120ml/4fl oz/½ cup brown veal stock
25g/1oz/1½ tablespoons whole-grain mustard
salt and freshly milled pepper
oil for frying
sprigs of fresh herbs to garnish

Heat half the oil and sweat 50g/2oz/⅓ cup of the onion until translucent. Add the garlic and sweat for a further minute. Leave to cool, then add the veal trimmings and mince (grind) through a coarse mincer plate, or work in a food processor. Work in the egg and then half the cream. Season generously and shape into 20 small burgers.

For the sauce, sweat the remaining onion in the remaining oil, then add the peppercorns and white wine and reduce by two-thirds by fast boiling. Add the veal stock and remaining cream and reduce by fast boiling to a thick sauce consistency. Pass through a fine sieve. Stir in the mustard and season to taste.

Fry the burgers in a little oil for about 4 minutes on each side until golden brown. Alternatively, grill (broil) them for 7-8 minutes, turning once. Garnish and serve warm with the mustard sauce for dipping.

PHOTOGRAPH ON PAGE 82

MEDITERRANEAN NUGGETS

The combination of flavours incorporated in these tiny meatballs is classic of Arab influences in the Southern Mediterranean – enhanced by the saffron mayonnaise.

MAKES 40

450g/1lb/2 cups finely minced (ground) beef
or lamb
2 shallots, finely chopped
2 cloves of garlic, crushed
25g/1oz/½ cup coriander (cilantro) leaves,
finely chopped
1 teaspoon ground cumin
100g/4oz/½ cup stoned (pitted) green olives,
finely chopped
2 teaspoons beaten egg
½ teaspoon salt
½ teaspoon freshly milled pepper
2 tablespoons vegetable oil
saffron mayonnaise (see page 137)

Combine all the ingredients except the oil and shape into 40 small balls.

Place in a roasting tin (pan) with the oil and bake in a preheated oven at 190°C/375°F/gas mark 5 for 15 minutes until well browned. Serve at once with saffron mayonnaise.

PHOTOGRAPH ON PAGE 82

WINGLETS WITH
BARBECUE SAUCE

This is good fun food, great for outdoor eating.

MAKES 20

20 chicken winglets
50ml/2fl oz/¼ cup light soy sauce
120ml/4fl oz/½ cup natural yoghurt
oil for deep frying

For the sauce:
25g/1oz/2 tablespoons unsalted butter
2 tablespoons vegetable oil
50g/2oz/⅓ cup onion, finely chopped
½ teaspoon black peppercorns, crushed
1 chilli, chopped
120ml/4fl oz/½ cup dry white wine
250ml/8fl oz/1 cup veal or chicken stock
120ml/4fl oz/½ cup tomato ketchup
1 teaspoon freshly grated root ginger
2 teaspoons freshly grated horseradish
salt

Discard the pointed end of each chicken winglet. Using a small sharp knife, scrape the flesh off the bones and push it back over the thicker end of the joint.

Discard the thin second bone. Repeat until all the winglets are prepared in this way.

Combine the soy sauce and yoghurt and marinate the chicken winglets for up to 24 hours in a cool place.

For the sauce, heat the butter and oil and sweat the onion and peppercorns until the onion is translucent. Add the chilli and sweat for a further minute. Add the wine and reduce by three-quarters by fast boiling. Add the stock, ketchup, ginger and horseradish. Simmer to a medium thick consistency, then pass through a fine sieve. Season to taste with salt.

Drain the chicken winglets thoroughly. Heat the oil and deep fry the pieces of chicken until golden brown and well cooked. Drain on absorbent paper and serve with the sauce.

LEFT TO RIGHT:
MEDITERRANEAN NUGGET · MARINATED CHICKEN ALANYA
VEAL BITKIS · WINGLETS WITH BARBECUE SAUCE
SCAMPI TAILS WITH RED CURRY SAUCE · THAI CURRY BITES

GOLDEN TRIANGLES

MAKES ABOUT 20

175g/6oz puff pastry
1 egg beaten
100g/4oz/½ cup peeled prawns or
shrimps, chopped
50ml/2fl oz/¼ cup double (heavy) cream
50ml/2fl oz/¼ cup dry white wine
1 teaspoon freshly grated ginger
1 red chilli, seeds removed and finely diced
cayenne
salt and freshly milled pepper
dill sprigs to garnish

On a lightly floured surface, roll out the pastry about 3mm/⅛ inch thick and cut out about 20 5cm/2 inch triangles. Using a small sharp knife, mark a lattice on each triangle. Brush with beaten egg and leave to rest in a cool place for at least 20 minutes.

Bake in a preheated oven at 220°C/425°F/gas mark 7 for abut 15 minutes until risen and golden brown. Cool on a wire tray.

Season the prawns or shrimps and cook quickly in the cream and white wine, remove from the pan and keep to one side. Add the ginger and chilli to the cream and reduce by fast boiling until very thick.

Purée the prawns and the reduced cream in a food processor and season to taste.

Split the pastry triangles in half and sandwich together with a little of the prawn mixture. Serve at once, garnished with small sprigs of dill.

SPICY VINE LEAVES

MAKES 30

400g/14oz/scant 2 cups pork tenderloin, cut in
small dice
salt and freshly milled pepper
2 tablespoons oil
15g/½oz/1 tablespoon unsalted butter
2 tablespoons finely chopped onion
2 cloves of garlic, crushed
2 chillies, finely chopped
25g/1oz/3 tablespoons pine kernels
2 dessert apples, peeled, cored and
finely chopped
1 teaspoon freshly grated root ginger
120ml/4fl oz/½ cup dry white wine
30 vine leaves preserved in brine
chicken stock

Season the pork with salt and pepper. Heat the oil and butter in a frying pan and quickly fry the pork until browned on all sides. Remove from the pan.

Add the onion to the pan and sweat until translucent, then add the garlic and cook for a further minute. Add the chillies, pine kernels, apple and ginger, then return the pork to the pan and add the wine. Cook quickly for about 5 minutes until all the liquid has evaporated. Leave to cool. Season to taste.

Thoroughly wash the vine leaves, then lay them out on a kitchen cloth (dish towel) and pat dry. Place a spoonful of filling on each leaf, then fold in the sides and roll each one to enclose the filling.

Place the vine leaf rolls in an ovenproof dish and moisten with a little hot chicken stock. Cover and cook in a preheated oven at 180°C/350°F/gas mark 4 for about 10 minutes until heated through. Serve warm.

GULLS' EGGS
À LA SOPHIE

Gulls' eggs have a short season from about the end of April to the end of May. They must be bought from a licensed dealer and are best bought ready-cooked as a lot of shells may have hairline cracks that cause them to burst open when boiled. Gulls' eggs are delicious served traditionally with celery and oriental salts but they can also be incorporated in salads and canapés. Quails' eggs are a good substitute when gulls' eggs are out of season.

Hop shoots are available within the asparagus season; if unobtainable, use young English asparagus tips.

MAKES 20

5 boiled gulls' eggs
20 slices of French bread, toasted
50g/2oz/4 tablespoons unsalted butter
100g/4oz hop shoots
celery and oriental salts

Peel the gulls' eggs and cut in slices using an egg slicer.

Spread the bread lightly with butter. Melt the remaining butter and toss the hop shoots. Place a small amount on each slice of bread, then top with slices of gulls' egg. Sprinkle with celery and oriental salts.

VEGETABLE AND CHILLI CRÊPES

MAKES ABOUT 40

For the crêpes:

200g/7oz/1⅔ cups plain (all-purpose) flour
1 teaspoon curry powder
¼ teaspoon chilli powder
500ml/18fl oz/2 cups milk
100g/4oz/½ cup sweetcorn kernels
20g/¾oz/⅓ cup freshly chopped herbs such as parsley and coriander (cilantro)
4 eggs
salt and freshly milled pepper
oil or clarified butter for frying

For the filling:

4 plum tomatoes, skinned, seeds removed and diced
75g/3oz/⅓ cup cucumber, skinned, seeds removed and diced
75g/3oz/⅓ cup white radish, diced
75g/3oz/⅓ cup celery, skinned and diced
75g/3oz/⅓ cup red pepper, skinned and diced
4 spring onions (scallions), chopped
40g/1½oz/¼ cup hazelnuts, chopped
50ml/2fl oz/¼ cup crème fraîche
50ml/2fl oz/¼ cup mayonnaise (see page 137)
50ml/2fl oz/¼ cup tomato ketchup
1 teaspoon freshly chopped coriander (cilantro)
1 teaspoon freshly grated horseradish

Combine all the ingredients for the crêpes and beat to give a fairly smooth batter. Use the mixture to make about 30 miniature crêpes, about 10cm/4 inch in diameter. Keep warm.

Mix all the ingredients for the filling together and season to taste. Spoon a small amount of filling in the centre of each crêpe, fold in half and then in half again. Serve at once.

SCAMPI TAILS WITH RED CURRY SAUCE

Another delightful Thai dish, very spicy yet very smooth on the tongue – a real experience. Traditionally seafood is served with a red curry sauce whilst meat dishes are served with a green curry sauce. Scallops or firm white fish such as monkfish may be cooked in the same way.

MAKES 40

40 shelled scampi tails or raw prawns (shrimp)
150ml/¼ pint/⅔ cup olive oil
40ml/1½fl oz/2⅔ tablespoons light soy sauce
3 coriander (cilantro) stalks, finely chopped
1 clove of garlic, crushed
1 teaspoon freshly grated root ginger
1 stalk of lemon grass, finely chopped

For the sauce:

1 tablespoon vegetable oil
3 long red chillies, seeds removed and chopped
25g/1oz/3 tablespoons shallots, finely chopped
1 clove of garlic, crushed
1 stalk of lemon grass, finely chopped
2 coriander (cilantro) stalks, finely chopped
150ml/¼ pint/⅔ cup coconut milk
100g/4oz/½ cup cream of coconut
150ml/¼ pint/⅔ cup of double (heavy) cream
¼ teaspoon shrimp paste
6 green peppercorns, crushed
salt

Cut the scampi tails or prawns along their length and remove any dark intestine. Wash and dry them thoroughly.

Combine the olive oil, soy sauce, coriander stalks, garlic, ginger and lemon grass in a bowl. Add the scampi tails, cover and leave in a cool place to marinate for up to 24 hours.

For the sauce, heat the oil and sweat the chillies, shallots, garlic, lemon grass and coriander. Add the coconut milk, cream of coconut and cream, then stir in the shrimp paste and peppercorns. Simmer for 10 minutes, cool slightly, then purée in a liquidiser (blender) and pass through a fine sieve. Season with salt to taste. Add the scampi tails or prawns to the sauce and simmer for 3-5 minutes until just cooked.

Lift the scampi tails or prawns from the sauce and place a cocktail stick (toothpick) in each one. Arrange on a serving dish and spoon a little sauce over or serve separately as a dipping sauce.

PHOTOGRAPH ON PAGE 82

GAMBAS WITH SAGE LEAVES

SKEWERS
A N D
Wrappers

This chapter is truly international, bringing colour and excitement from all corners of the world. The variation of ingredients can be fully exploited and the presentation made stunning. It occurred to us that there's very little that cannot be skewered, and the few things that cannot be threaded on a skewer we simply wrapped.

More than a few of the exceptional dishes in this chapter – such as Langoustines in their Pyjamas with Mango Sauce, Salmon Pasties (an old British idea), assorted Satay from Thailand and Prawn Rolls from China – show a wonderful contrast of style, flavour and textures. It would be so easy to shape an interesting cocktail party menu around skewers and wrappers alone. With some imagination, the possibilities are endless.

DON GIOVANNI

If you can't find the required ingredients
why not come into The Savoy to try one
of these newly created cocktails by
Peter Dorelli, Head Barman.

⅙ Wachauer Marillen
⅙ Alpen Krauter
⅙ peach liqueur
½ passion fruit nectar
3 dashes of crème de cassis

Shake with ice. Decorate with three
raspberries.

GAMBAS WITH SAGE LEAVES

A macho canapé! Use langoustines as an alternative.

MAKES 20

10 rashers (slices) of streaky bacon
40 sage leaves
20 raw prawns (shrimp), peeled and de-veined
20 button mushrooms
oil for deep frying
rouille to serve (see page 133)

Remove the rind from the bacon and with the back of a knife, stretch each rasher. Cut each rasher in half crossways.

Place 2 sage leaves on each prawn, then wrap a piece of bacon around each one. Thread a mushroom, then a prawn on to each of 20 skewers.

Heat the oil over a medium heat and deep fry the skewers until the bacon is golden and the prawns are pink. Drain on absorbent paper and serve with rouille handed separately.

PHOTOGRAPH ON PAGE 86

HUNGARIAN WRAPPERS

The flavour and character of a great culture is embodied in these little wrappers from the Hungarian *puszta* famous for its sweet peppers and paprika.

MAKES ABOUT 20

1 tablespoon vegetable oil
15g/½oz/1 tablespoon unsalted butter
50g/2oz/⅓ cup onion, finely chopped
2 cloves of garlic, crushed
1 green chilli, seeds removed and finely chopped
150g/5oz/heaped ½ cup lean minced (ground) pork
2 teaspoons paprika
1½ teaspoons tomato purée (paste)
3 tablespoons double (heavy) cream
25g/1oz/1½ tablespoons long-grain rice, boiled and drained
2 teaspoons freshly chopped marjoram or oregano
salt and freshly milled pepper
about 20 sweet cherry peppers in brine, thoroughly drained.

Heat the oil and butter and sweat the onions until translucent. Add the garlic and chilli and sweat for a further minute. Stir in the minced pork and fry for 2 minutes until well browned on all sides. Stir in the paprika, tomato purée, cream, cooked rice and herbs and cook gently, stirring until well mixed. Season to taste.

Make a small split in the side of each cherry pepper and fill with a little of the mixture.

Place in a buttered baking dish and heat in a preheated oven at 200°C/400°F/gas mark 6 for 5 minutes until warmed. Serve at once.

CHICKEN SKEWERS WITH BACON

Annual visits to the Okura Hotel in Japan have been inspiring. This canapé was made in the idiom of the delightful morsels prepared for waiting customers at Yakitori stands.

MAKES 40

200g/7oz skinless and boneless chicken breast
200g/7oz chicken or turkey livers
10 rashers (slices) of streaky bacon
½ quantity chicken farce (see page 134)
40 quail's eggs
40 each bay leaves and sage leaves
salt and freshly milled pepper
vegetable oil or melted butter to glaze
Japanese pickled ginger to serve

Cut the chicken in 40 small cubes. Cut the chicken livers in 40 small pieces. Season both with salt and pepper.

Remove the rind from the bacon and cut each rasher in half lengthways and crossways. Wrap a piece of bacon around each piece of chicken liver.

Using floured hands, roll the chicken farce in 40 small balls.

Cook the quails' eggs in boiling salted water for 3 minutes. Drain and refresh in iced water. Drain and peel.

Thread each bamboo skewer with a ball of farce, a piece of bacon-wrapped liver, a quail's egg, a bay leaf, a sage leaf and a piece of chicken. Brush lightly with vegetable oil and cook under a preheated grill for about 5 minutes. Serve at once with Japanese pickled ginger.

PHOTOGRAPH ON PAGE 91

FETA, OLIVE AND SALAMI STICKS

MAKES 20

225 g/8oz Feta cheese
10 pickled chillies, quartered
20 thin slices of salami, halved
20 green olives stuffed with pimento
20 small black olives, stoned (pitted)

Cut the Feta cheese in 40 small cubes and wrap a piece of chilli around each cube.

Fold each piece of salami and thread two on to each skewer with one green and one black olive and two cubes of cheese.

PASTRAMI AND PICKLES

Typically New York fast food, uncomplicated, honest and full of flavour.

MAKES 20

225g/8oz pastrami in one piece
2 medium-sized pickled cucumbers in sweet and sour vinegar
10 pickled baby sweetcorn (corn), halved
20 pickled silverskin onions

Cut the pastrami in 40 small cubes. Cut each cucumber in 10 slices.

Thread two pieces of pastrami, a slice of cucumber, a piece of sweetcorn and an onion on each skewer.

HAM AND ASPARAGUS KISSES

A novel way of eating asparagus – the Parma ham adds a gorgeous flavour to the unique taste of asparagus. For a special occasion use the tips only.

MAKES 20

20 asparagus spears
10 slices of Parma ham (prosciutto)
unsalted butter, melted
salt and freshly milled pepper
mayonnaise (see page 137) flavoured with freshly shredded basil leaves to serve

Peel the asparagus spears, then tie in a bundle and blanch in boiling salted water. Drain and refresh in iced water. Cut each asparagus spear in four short even-sized lengths. Cut each slice of ham in eight strips and wrap one around each piece of asparagus.

Thread four pieces on to each bamboo skewer. Brush with melted butter and season with pepper. Cook under a pre-heated grill (broiler), turning once, for about 3 minutes.

Serve at once with mayonnaise flavoured with basil leaves.

LEFT TO RIGHT:
CHICKEN SKEWERS WITH BACON · GAMBAS WITH SAGE LEAVES
HAM AND ASPARAGUS KISSES · PIGEON TIKKA
FETA, OLIVE AND SALAMI STICKS · PASTRAMI AND PICKLES

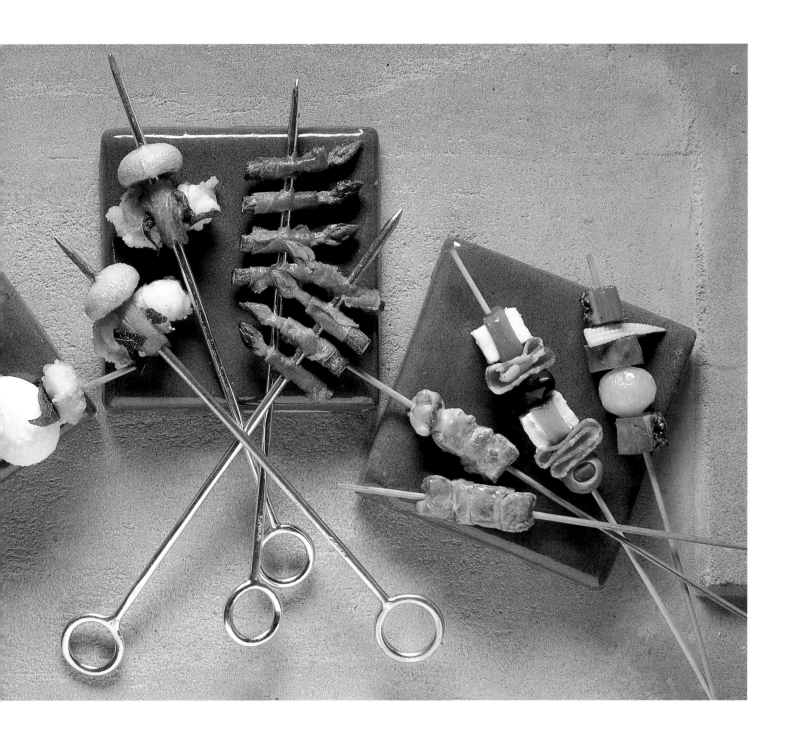

PICKLED SKEWERS

A skewer for the summer to be eaten in the warm sun with an aperitif.

MAKES 20

150g/5oz Tallegio or Bel Paese cheese
5 pickled or marinated peppers
5 small slices of smoked ham
20 small olives
20 pickled silverskin onions

Cut the cheese in 20 small cubes.

Cut along one side of each pepper, trim and flatten it. Place on a kitchen cloth (dish towel) and remove excess moisture.

Place a pepper on each slice of ham, then roll up and cut in four slices. Thread a ham and pepper pinwheel on each skewer with a piece of cheese, an olive and a silverskin onion.

SALMON PASTIES

Why are pasties made with minced meat – salmon makes much more sense!

MAKES ABOUT 30

15g/½oz/1 tablespoon unsalted butter
1 tablespoon finely chopped shallot
15g/½oz/1 tablespoon carrot, finely diced and blanched
15g/½oz/1 tablespoon swede (rutabaga) or turnip, finely diced and blanched
salt and freshly milled pepper
120ml/4fl oz/½ cup dry white wine
4 tablespoons double (heavy) cream
100g/4oz/½ cup salmon fillet, diced
1 teaspoon freshly chopped basil
350g/12oz shortcrust pastry (see page 138)
beaten egg to glaze

Melt the butter and sweat the shallot until translucent. Add the vegetables and season with salt and pepper. Add the white wine and reduce. Add the cream and reduce until very thick. Remove from the heat and add the salmon. Stir in the basil and season to taste. Leave to cool.

On a lightly floured surface, roll out the pastry thinly and stamp out about 30 6.5cm/2½ inch plain rounds. Brush each with a little beaten egg and place a small spoonful of filling on each. Draw up the sides of the pastry and press together to seal well. Crimp the top edge of each pasty. Leave to rest in a cool place for at least 20 minutes.

Place on a baking tray, brush lightly with beaten egg and bake in a preheated oven at 200°C/400°F/gas mark 6 for 10-15 minutes until golden. Serve warm.

PIGEON TIKKA

Full of flavour, strong pigeon meat can take on bold spices. Chicken or duck may also be used in this recipe. Start with 1lb/450g boneless and skinless chicken or duck breast.

MAKES ABOUT 40

4 wood pigeons
300ml/½ pint/1¼ cups natural yoghurt
1 tablespoon ground cashew nuts or ground almonds
1 tablespoon vegetable oil
juice of 1 lemon
2 cloves of garlic, crushed
½ teaspoon garam masala
½ teaspoon cardamom powder
pinch of turmeric
½ teaspoon salt

Remove the breasts from each wood pigeon and discard the skin. The carcasses may be used to make stock.

Cut each breast in 1.5cm/½-¾ inch dice and place in a bowl. Combine all the remaining ingredients and add to the pieces of pigeon. Mix well to coat each piece evenly. Cover and marinate in a cool place for at least 12 hours.

Thread four pieces of pigeon on to bamboo skewers and cook under a pre-heated grill for 3-4 minutes, turning occasionally. Serve at once.

PHOTOGRAPH ON PAGE 91

LETTUCE SATCHELS

Use a firm leaf such as escarole, webb's, or batavia.

MAKES 20

20 medium lettuce leaves
25g/1oz/2 tablespoons unsalted butter
75g/3oz/½ cup chicken livers, chopped
2 plum tomatoes, peeled, seeds removed and diced
4 spring onions (scallions), cut in small julienne
salt and freshly milled pepper
melted butter to glaze

Drop the lettuce leaves into boiling salted water, then drain immediately and refresh in iced water. Drain and dry thoroughly on a kitchen cloth (dish towel).

Melt the butter in a frying pan. Season the chicken livers and seal quickly in the hot butter. Remove from the heat, add the tomatoes and spring onion and toss quickly. Season to taste.

Spoon a little of the mixture on to each lettuce leaf and roll up, folding in the sides of each leaf to completely enclose the filling. Brush with a little melted butter and place in a baking dish. Cover and warm through in a preheated oven at 200°C/400°F/gas mark 6 for 2-3 minutes. Serve warm.

PRAWN AND BAMBOO SHOOT WONTON

Easy to make and a sure success with your guests – for a laugh try serving them with chopsticks!

Wonton wrappers are available from Chinese and Thai supermarkets. If you can't get them substitute filo pastry.

MAKES ABOUT 40

1 tablespoon vegetable oil
1 tablespoon chopped shallot
1 clove of garlic, crushed
½ teaspoon grated root ginger
5 spring onions (scallions), chopped
200g/7oz/1 cup peeled cooked prawns (shrimp), chopped
50g/2oz/⅓ cup bamboo shoots, chopped
1 teaspoon light soy sauce
½ teaspoon oyster sauce
about 40 wonton wrappers
oil for deep frying

Heat the oil in a wok or frying pan and sweat the shallots very quickly, then add the garlic, ginger and spring onions and fry for about 1 minute, stirring constantly.
Add the prawns, bamboo shoots, soy and oyster sauces and cool slightly.

Place a teaspoonful of the mixture in the centre of each wonton wrapper. Brush the edges with water, then draw them up to the centre and press tightly to seal.

Heat the oil and deep fry the wonton until crisp and golden. Drain on absorbent paper. Serve warm.

PRAWN (SHRIMP) ROLLS

Spring roll wrappers are available from Chinese and Thai supermarkets and may be used instead of filo pastry.

MAKES ABOUT 30

450g/1lb peeled cooked prawns (shrimp), finely chopped
2 teaspoons fish sauce
2 teaspoons soy sauce
2 teaspoons grated root ginger
4 teaspoons finely chopped spring onion (scallion)
freshly milled pepper
8 large sheets of filo pastry
oil for deep frying

Combine the prawns, fish and soy sauces, ginger and spring onion. Season with pepper to taste.

Quarter each sheet of filo pastry crossways and place a spoonful of filling in the centre. Roll each one up, folding in the sides to make a neat roll.

Deep fry in hot oil until crisp and golden. Drain on absorbent paper. Serve at once.

SATAY

MAKES ABOUT 20

225g/8oz skinless and boneless chicken
225g/8oz lean fillet of lamb or fillet of beef
1 tablespoon sesame or poppy seeds

For the marinade:
150ml/¼ pint/⅔ cup groundnut oil
1 tablespoon light soy sauce
3 tablespoons coconut milk
1 clove of garlic, crushed
1 teaspoon finely chopped coriander
(cilantro) stalks

For the satay sauce:
100g/4oz/⅔ cup peanuts, skinned
150ml/¼ pint/⅔ cup coconut milk
2 tablespoons pineapple juice
1 tablespoon soft light brown sugar
1 teaspoon red curry paste
¼ teaspoon salt

Cut the chicken and lamb (or beef) in small dice about 1cm/⅜ inch. Place in separate bowls.

Combine the ingredients for the marinade and pour half over each meat. Toss well, then cover and marinate in a cool place for up to 24 hours.

Remove the meat from the marinade and thread several pieces on each bamboo skewer. Sprinkle with seeds. Cook under a preheated grill (broiler) for about 5 minutes until lightly browned.

For the sauce, roast the peanuts in a preheated oven at 200°C/400°F/gas mark 6 for about 15 minutes until golden. Cool and grind until fairly smooth in a food processor or coffee grinder. Combine with the remaining ingredients in a small saucepan. Bring to the boil stirring, then simmer for 2–3 minutes. Serve the skewers with the sauce handed separately.

ROUNDS OF PORK IN GOLDEN THREADS

Minced pork with ginger wrapped in fine soft noodles, deep fried then dipped in chilli sauce before eating – truly Thai. Other white meats such as veal, chicken or turkey may also be substituted.

MAKES ABOUT 40

2 tablespoons vegetable oil
50g/2oz/⅓ cup shallots, chopped
2 cloves of garlic, crushed
2 teaspoons freshly grated root ginger
50g/2oz/½ cup mushrooms, chopped
225g/8oz/1¼ cups lean pork, diced
12 stalks of fresh coriander (cilantro), chopped
salt and freshly milled pepper
25g/1oz/⅓ cup dried or 75g/3oz/¾ cup fresh
thin egg noodles
1 egg yolk
oil for deep frying
chilli sauce for dipping

Heat the oil and sweat the shallots, garlic, ginger and mushrooms until the shallot is translucent. Add the pork and coriander and cook over a medium heat for 2–3 minutes until the pork is cooked. Season to taste.

Allow the mixture to cool, then pass through a fine mincer (grinder) or work in a food processor until finely minced. Shape into about 40 balls, pressing firmly so that the mixture holds together.

Cook the dried noodles in boiling salted water until just cooked, then drain and refresh in iced water. Drain and lay out on a clean kitchen (dish) towel to absorb the moisture. Mix with the egg yolk. If using fresh noodles there is no need to cook them first.

Wrap a thread of noodle around each pork ball. Heat the oil and fry the balls until golden. Drain on absorbent paper. Serve warm with chilli sauce for dipping.

ROUNDS OF PORK IN GOLDEN THREADS
SATAY

ITALIAN CHEESE AND ONION MARMALADE ENVELOPES

Torta is a wonderful Italian invention – a mixture of gorgonzola and rich creamy mascarpone layered together to produce a powerful yet smooth 'cake' of cheese.

MAKES 40

20g/³⁄₄oz/1¹⁄₂ tablespoons unsalted butter
2 tablespoons olive oil
3 medium-sized red onions, chopped
sprig of thyme
50ml/2fl oz/¹⁄₄ cup white wine vinegar
250ml/8fl oz/1 cup dry white wine
1 tablespoon honey
salt and freshly milled pepper
450g/1lb Torta cheese
8 large sheets of filo pastry
egg white to glaze
seeds to sprinkle such as sesame or linseed
oil for deep frying

Heat the butter and oil in a large saucepan and sweat the onions until translucent. Add the sprig of thyme and wine vinegar and reduce by half by fast boiling. Add the white wine and reduce completely. Stir in the honey and season to taste. Leave to cool.

Cut the cheese in 40 thin half-slices. Cut each sheet of filo pastry in five short strips.

Place one piece of cheese and a small amount of the onion marmalade on each strip of filo pastry. Fold a small strip of pastry in along both long edges, then starting at a short end fold the pastry over to enclose the filling completely. Brush with a little egg white to seal the end. Make the remaining envelopes in the same way.

Brush each filo envelope lightly with egg white and sprinkle with seeds. Deep fry in hot oil until crisp and golden. Drain on absorbent paper. Serve warm.

MUSTARD-GLAZED SWEETCORN (CORN)

MAKES 30

30 miniature sweetcorn (corn)
1 shallot, finely chopped
25g/1oz/2 tablespoons unsalted butter
¹⁄₂ teaspoon mustard seeds
2 tablespoons soft light brown sugar
2 tablespoons fresh orange juice
freshly milled pepper

Place the sweetcorn in a saucepan of boiling salted water and bring to the boil again. Drain and refresh in iced water. Drain and dry thoroughly.

Lightly sauté the shallot in the butter, then add the remaining ingredients.

Place the sweetcorn in a roasting tin (pan) and pour the sauce over the sweetcorn. Cook in a preheated oven at 200°C/400°F/gas mark 6 for 5-7 minutes until well glazed. Shake the tin from time to time. Serve at once threaded on to small bamboo skewers or cocktail sticks (toothpicks).

GINGERED MONKFISH TWISTERS

A most unusual twist of cheese and monkfish which needs to be cooked quickly and eaten quickly.

MAKES 30

400g/14oz monkfish fillet, well trimmed
50ml/2fl oz/¹⁄₄ cup light soy sauce
2 teaspoons freshly grated ginger
4 tablespoons freshly chopped coriander
(cilantro)
175g/6oz Emmenthal cheese
30 cherry tomatoes
salt and freshly milled pepper
freshly chopped coriander (cilantro) to garnish

Cut the monkfish in 60 even-sized pieces. Combine the soy sauce, ginger and coriander and marinate the fish for at least 1 hour in a cool place.

Cut the Emmenthal cheese in 30 even-sized cubes.

Thread each skewer with a cherry tomato, a cube of fish, a cube of cheese and a second cube of fish. Cook the skewers under a preheated grill (broiler) on the hottest setting for about 2 minutes until the fish is just cooked.

Serve warm sprinkled with freshly chopped coriander.

ANGELS ON HORSEBACK

A delightful name for a delightful little dish. Traditionally oysters were only available in the winter, during the months with an 'r' in them, but now farmed oysters are available all year round. Look for Irish ones, which are particularly good.

MAKES 20

20 oysters
10 rashers (slices) of streaky bacon
5 slices of brown bread
unsalted butter for spreading
10g/¼oz/2 tablespoons parsley sprigs, washed
and thoroughly dried
oil for deep frying
salt and freshly milled pepper

Open the oysters and remove them from the half shell.

Remove the rind from the bacon and with the back of a knife, stretch each rasher until it is very thin. Cut each rasher in half and wrap a piece around each oyster.

Thread the oysters on to 20 skewers and cook under a hot grill (broiler), turning occasionally, until the bacon is crisp.

Toast the bread and spread lightly with butter. Cut out 20 long thin triangles and place a skewer on each piece of toast.

Drop the parsley in hot oil, then remove instantly and place on a kitchen cloth (dish towel). Season with salt and pepper and sprinkle over the oysters.

VEGETABLE SAMOSAS

These delightful spicy vegetable cushions are a must at every cocktail party. The pineapple adds a little twist of sweetness to the spice.

Filo pastry dries very quickly once it is unwrapped so lay it out flat and keep it in a large polythene bag covered with a damp kitchen cloth. Take out one sheet at a time to work with.

The samosas may be shaped and left on a tray covered with polythene in the refrigerator until required. They should always be cooked just before serving.

MAKES ABOUT 30

2 tablespoons oil
20g/¾oz/1½ tablespoons unsalted butter
2 tablespoons finely chopped onion
1 clove of garlic, crushed
1 chilli, seeds removed and finely chopped
1 teaspoon curry powder
¼ teaspoon cardamom powder
200g/7oz/1½ cups potato, diced and cooked
al dente
50g/2oz/⅓ cup green beans, cooked al dente
and diced
50g/2oz/½ cup carrot, diced
50g/2oz/⅓ cup sweetcorn kernels
50g/2oz/⅓ cup broccoli stalk, diced
50g/2oz/⅓ cup pineapple, diced
salt and freshly milled pepper
cayenne
4 large sheets of filo pastry
oil for deep frying
plum sauce to serve

Heat the oil and butter in a frying pan and sweat the onion until translucent. Add the garlic, chilli, curry powder and cardamom powder and sweat for a further minute. Stir in the vegetables and pineapple and cook for 1-2 minutes over a medium heat. Season to taste with salt, pepper and cayenne. Leave to cool.

Cut each sheet of filo in eight short strips and place a small amount of filling at one end of each strip. Fold the pastry over at an angle to cover the filling, then continue folding to make a triangular parcel. Repeat with all the remaining strips to make 32 parcels.

Heat the oil and deep fry the parcels until crisp and golden. Drain on absorbent paper. Serve warm with plum sauce.

PHOTOGRAPH ON PAGE 98

LEEK AND HAM CROISSANTS

Puff pastry can be used as a quick alternative to the yeast dough for these mini croissants with a difference. Any number of fillings may be substituted – try grated cheese or finely diced spicy sausage.

MAKES 20

For the dough:
20g/³/₄oz/1 cake fresh yeast
4 tablespoons lukewarm water
100ml/3½ fl oz/scant ½ cup vegetable oil
pinch of sugar
pinch of salt
250g/9oz/heaped 2 cups strong (bread) plain flour, sifted

For the filling:
25g/1oz/2 tablespoons unsalted butter
75g/3oz/½ cup leek, finely chopped
75g/3oz/7 tablespoons cooked ham, finely chopped
½ teaspoon freshly chopped sage
salt and freshly milled pepper
beaten egg to glaze
caraway, poppy or sesame seeds to sprinkle

Mix the yeast with the water until evenly combined. Add the yeast liquid, oil, sugar and salt to the flour and mix well for about 5 minutes. Form the dough into a ball, cover and leave to rest for 15 minutes at room temperature.

For the filling, melt the butter and sweat the leek until soft. Add the ham and sage and season generously. Cook until all the liquid has been absorbed. Cool.

Roll out the dough on a lightly floured surface to a rectangle measuring 40 × 30cm/16 × 12 inches, then cut in four strips measuring 30 × 10cm/12 × 4 inches. Cut out five triangles from each strip of pastry, each triangle measuring 10cm/4 inches across the base.

Place a little filling at the base of each triangle and roll up. Twist the ends around to meet to form croissants. Place the croissants on a lightly greased baking sheet. Leave to rest in a cool place for at least 20 minutes. Brush them with beaten egg and sprinkle with caraway seeds. Bake in a preheated oven at 200°C/400°F/gas mark 6 for about 20 minutes until golden. Serve warm.

MONEYBAGS

Moneybags are a regular feature on cocktail party menus at The Savoy. They can be prepared in advance ready to be fried at the last moment.

MAKES ABOUT 10

For the egg white pancakes:
4 egg whites
50ml/2fl oz/¼ cup water
2 teaspoons cornflour
oil for frying

For the filling:
25g/1oz/2 tablespoons unsalted butter
2 teaspoons finely chopped shallot
100g/4oz/1 cup wild mushrooms, trimmed and finely chopped
40g/1½oz/2½ tablespoons raw chicken breast, finely chopped
50ml/2fl oz/¼ cup double (heavy) cream
1 tablespoon freshly chopped parsley
salt and freshly milled pepper
8-10 chive stalks, blanched

For the pancakes, mix the egg whites, water and cornflour together thoroughly. Use this mixture to make eight to ten 15cm/6 inch diameter pancakes in the usual way.

For the filling, melt the butter and sweat the shallot, mushrooms and chicken. Stir in the cream and cook until the mixture is thickened. Stir in the parsley and season to taste.

Divide the filling between the pancakes, then draw up the edges of each one and tie the tops with chive stalks. Cut away any excess pancake above the ties.

Deep fry the 'moneybags' in hot oil until crisp. Drain on absorbent kitchen paper and serve at once.

CLOCKWISE:
SPRING ROLLS WITH DUCK AND CHILLIES
MONEYBAGS
VEGETABLE SAMOSAS
LEEK AND HAM CROISSANTS

SAVOY CABBAGE PARCELS

A very aptly named cabbage when all is said and done. Its attractively veined leaves make a perfect wrapping.

MAKES ABOUT 30

8 large pale green leaves from a Savoy cabbage
25g/1oz/2 tablespoons unsalted butter
2 tablespoons vegetable oil
1 small shallot, finely chopped
25g/1oz/1-2 slices back (lean) bacon, cut in julienne and blanched
100g/4oz/1 cup chanterelles (or other wild mushrooms)
25g/1oz/¼ cup morels (or other wild mushrooms)
50ml/2fl oz/¼ cup double (heavy) cream
65g/2½oz/heaped 1 cup fresh white breadcrumbs
2 egg yolks
1 egg, beaten
3 tablespoons freshly chopped parsley
salt and freshly milled pepper
chicken stock for poaching
green herb sauce to serve (see page 137)

Blanch the cabbage leaves in boiling salted water, then drain and refresh in iced water. Place the leaves on a kitchen cloth (dish towel) and dry thoroughly. Cut away the thick central stalk from each leaf.

Heat the butter and oil and sweat the shallot until translucent, then add the bacon and sweat for a further minute. Wash and trim the mushrooms carefully, then slice and add to the pan and sweat for about 2 minutes.

Remove the pan from the heat and stir in the cream, then add the breadcrumbs and eggs and cook over a very gentle heat, stirring until thickened. Stir in the parsley and season to taste.

Divide the mixture between the cabbage leaves and roll each one up. Wrap in foil or cling film and poach in chicken stock for 15-20 minutes until firm to the touch. Remove from the pan and leave to cool.

Unwrap and cut each roll in four pieces. Serve with green herb sauce.

LANGOUSTINES IN THEIR PYJAMAS WITH MANGO SAUCE

Invented at The Savoy, this is probably our most prized recipe. It is simple, has excellent texture and taste and combines the very best produce. It's easy to eat and very more-ish, especially with the mango sauce which goes so well you would think mangoes had been invented for this dish alone.

MAKES 20

1 litre/1¾ pint/4 cups fish or vegetable stock
20 live langoustines
3-4 large sheets of filo pastry
unsalted butter, melted
40 basil leaves
oil for deep frying

Bring the stock to the boil in a large saucepan. Add the langoustines and cook for 3 minutes. Drain and refresh in iced water.

Remove the tail meat from the shells and dry on a kitchen cloth (dish towel).

Cut out 20 10cm/4 inch squares of filo pastry and brush each with a little melted butter. Place two basil leaves and a langoustine tail on each. Roll up the pastry, twisting the ends together to seal them.

Heat the oil and deep fry the parcels until lightly golden. Drain on absorbent paper and serve at once with the mango sauce.

MANGO SAUCE

200g/7oz/1 large prepared ripe mango
5 hard-boiled egg yolks
300ml/½ pint/1¼ cups mayonnaise (see page 137)
2 tablespoons parsley, finely chopped
3 tablespoons basil leaves, finely sliced
salt and freshly milled pepper

Purée the mango with the hard-boiled egg yolks and mayonnaise. Pass through a fine sieve, then stir in the herbs. Season to taste.

CHICKEN AND SCALLOP TERIYAKI

Small queen scallops may be used instead of quartered whole scallops.

MAKES 40

200g/7oz chicken breast, skin and bones removed
1 red pepper
1 green pepper
10 scallops, cleaned and quartered
120ml/4fl oz/½ cup teriyaki sauce
250ml/8fl oz/1 cup orange juice
40g/1½oz/3 tablespoons soft light brown sugar
120ml/4fl oz/½ cup wine vinegar
salt and freshly milled pepper
5 spring onions (scallions), cut in julienne strips

Cut the chicken in 40 even pieces about 1.5cm/½ inch square. Core the peppers and cut each one in 40 similar-sized squares. Thread a piece of chicken, a piece of both red and green pepper and a quarter scallop on each skewer.

Combine the teriyaki sauce, orange juice, sugar and vinegar in a small saucepan and reduce by fast boiling until it thickens. Brush the skewers with this glaze and cook under a preheated grill (broiler) for 3-4 minutes until the chicken is just cooked.

Sprinkle with the spring onion julienne and serve at once.

SPRING ROLLS WITH DUCK AND CHILLIES

The crisp fragrant flavours of Asia are brought together in these delicious little rolls.

MAKES 40

50ml/2fl oz/¼ cup vegetable oil
1 medium-sized onion, thinly sliced
1 clove of garlic, crushed
2 green chillies, seeds removed and finely diced
1 teaspoon freshly grated root ginger
200g/7oz/1 cup boneless and skinless duck leg meat, finely diced
1 medium carrot, cut in short julienne
1 stick celery, cut in short julienne
2 spring onions (scallions), chopped
75g/3oz/1 cup kohlrabi, cut in short julienne
1 small red (sweet) pepper, seeds removed and finely diced
40g/1½oz/½ cup beansprouts
2 teaspoons soy sauce
1 teaspoon oyster sauce
1 teaspoon caster (superfine) sugar
1 teaspoon sesame oil
8 large sheets of filo pastry
beaten egg white to glaze
poppy seeds to sprinkle
oil for deep frying
light soy sauce for dipping

Heat the oil in a large frying pan or wok and add the onion, garlic, chillies and ginger. Stir-fry for 1 minute. Add the duck and fry over a high heat, stirring constantly, until the meat is browned on all sides.

Add all the remaining vegetables except the beansprouts and stir-fry for 1-2 minutes, then add the beansprouts. Stir in the soy and oyster sauces, sugar and sesame oil and leave to cool.

Cut each sheet of filo pastry in five short strips. Place a small amount of filling at one end of each strip, then fold in the long sides and roll up the pastry, starting at the short end, to completely enclose the filling. Seal the ends with a little beaten egg white. Brush each roll lightly with beaten egg white and sprinkle with poppy seeds.

Heat the oil and deep fry the rolls in batches until crisp and golden brown. Drain on absorbent paper.

Serve warm with light soy sauce for dipping.

PHOTOGRAPH ON PAGE 98

PÉRIGUEUX INDULGENCE

CRISP

AND

Crunchy

As the heading implies these canapés should not only appeal to four of the senses, but also to the fifth: they should sound good as well. In order to achieve this, cooking processes need to be fierce and short. When serving a selection of canapés from this section, do make sure that you serve them one at a time in order to retain the crispness and crunchiness intended.

There are old ideas re-vamped as well as new recipes in this chapter, but all of them are easy to prepare, and most of the work can be done in advance, with only the finishing touches to complete the dishes at the last moment.

The variation is great, and in this part of the book, perhaps more than any other, there should be a feeling of fun and lack of pretention – the main ingredients of an enjoyable party.

MAGIC PUNCH

This is traditionally made with a cone of sugar which
is placed in a holder over the saucepan of punch.
Warmed rum is then poured over the cone and set
alight gradually melting the sugar into the wine. You
can replace sugar cones with 250g/9oz sugar cubes
packed into a stainless steel sieve.

3 bottles of red wine
2 cloves
13cm/5 inch stick of cinnamon
grated rind and juice of 1 lemon
juice of 2 oranges
250g/9oz/1½ cups sugar cubes or a sugar cone
600ml/1 pint/2½ cups dark rum

Put the wine, spices and lemon rind into a large
saucepan and heat gently. Stir in the fruit juices.
Place the sugar in a stainless steel sieve and set it
across the top of the saucepan.
Warm the rum and gradually pour it over the
sugar, then set fire to it. Add more rum from time to
time to keep the flames alight. When all the sugar has
melted, stir the punch and serve.

PÉRIGUEUX INDULGENCE

This is the height of decadence. The merge of truffles and port is a special one, and once marinated the truffle produces a unique essence of unsurpassed flavour. It may be stored for several months and used to add that touch of luxury to almost any sauce.

MAKES 20

4 fresh truffles
about 150ml/¼ pint/⅔ cup ruby port
20 thin slices of baguette
unsalted butter for spreading
120ml/4fl oz/½ cup veal stock
25g/1oz/2 tablespoons unsalted butter
salt and freshly milled pepper

Brush the truffles well under cold running water. Dry them with a kitchen cloth (dish towel) and place in a small jar. Cover with the port and leave in a cool place for at least 24 hours.

Toast the baguette slices and spread them generously with butter.

Thinly slice the truffles. Combine the veal stock with 50ml/2fl oz/¼ cup of the port strained from the truffles – store the rest in a jar in the refrigerator – and reduce by fast boiling until a syrupy consistency is reached. Remove from the heat and whisk in the butter. Season to taste. Pass through a fine sieve.

Place the truffle slices in the hot sauce to warm through, then place a few on each slice of toast. Spoon a tiny amount of sauce on top and sprinkle with freshly milled pepper.

PHOTOGRAPH ON PAGE 102

PORTUGUESE FASHIONS

MAKES 40

10 small fresh sardines
2 tablespoons vegetable oil
120ml/4fl oz/½ cup extra virgin olive oil
25ml/1fl oz/2 tablespoons water
25ml/1fl oz/2 tablespoons red wine vinegar
1 tablespoon freshly chopped coriander
(cilantro)
pinch of sugar
salt and freshly milled pepper
2 small red onions, cut in thin rings
3 plum tomatoes, skinned, seeds
removed and diced
40 small fingers of olive bread, toasted
unsalted butter for spreading (optional)

Clean and wash the sardines thoroughly, then dry them and turn in the vegetable oil. Place under a preheated grill (broiler) and cook very quickly – 1 minute on each side. The sardines should not be completely cooked. Fillet each sardine, then cut the fillets in half crossways.

Mix together the olive oil, water, vinegar, coriander and sugar, and season to taste. Place the sardines in a single layer in a dish and cover with the marinade, onion rings and tomatoes. Cover and leave in the refrigerator for at least 4 hours.

Spread the olive bread with butter, if wished. Place a piece of sardine on each and garnish with a little onion and tomato.

FISH RIBBONS

The essence of this recipe lies in marinating the fish before coating and frying – the flavour is astounding.

MAKES ABOUT 20

200g/7oz fish fillets, skinned
juice of 1 lemon
1 teaspoon Worcestershire sauce
salt and freshly milled pepper
25g/1oz/3 tablespoons plain (all-purpose) flour
1 egg, beaten
75g/3oz/1¼ cups fresh white breadcrumbs
oil for deep frying
rouille to serve (see page 133)

Cut the fish in strips about 5cm/2 inches long and 1cm/⅜ inch wide. Place in a bowl with the lemon juice and Worcestershire sauce and season to taste. Cover and leave to marinate in a cool place for up to 30 minutes.

Drain the fish thoroughly and turn the strips in the flour, then the egg, and finally toss in breadcrumbs until evenly coated.

Heat the oil and fry the strips until crisp and golden, then drain on absorbent paper.

Serve at once with rouille handed separately.

BRIOCHE CROÛTES WITH APRICOT CHUTNEY AND GORGONZOLA

So simple, yet quite delicious!

MAKES 20

4 individual brioches
unsalted butter for spreading
20 teaspoons apricot chutney (see page 133)
100g/4oz Gorgonzola cheese

Cut each brioche in five slices and stamp out a neat shape from each slice, if wished. Toast the brioche lightly on both sides.

Spread the brioche generously with butter and spread 1 teaspoonful of chutney on each slice.

Crumble the cheese and place on top of the chutney.

TOP LEFT TO RIGHT:
SCALLOP CROÛTE WITH SAUCE VIERGE
WARM GOAT'S CHEESE IN A SEED CRUST
GARLIC AND HERB TOAST
TOMATO AND BEANSPROUT CROÛTE

REBLOCHON AND RADISH CROÛTES

The distinct flavour of Reblochon is admirably complemented by the fresh crispness of radish and shallot.

MAKES 20

1 Reblochon cheese
120ml/4fl oz/½ cup white wine vinegar
25ml/1fl oz/2 tablespoons water
120ml/4fl oz/½ cup olive oil
10 radishes, thinly sliced
20g/¾oz/2½ tablespoons shallot, thinly sliced
1 teaspoon freshly chopped parsley
½ teaspoon caraway seeds
20 slices of baguette
olive oil for frying
freshly milled pepper

Trim the rind from the Reblochon, then cut the cheese in thin slices.

Combine the vinegar, water, olive oil, radishes, shallot, parsley and caraway seeds. Add the cheese and season with pepper. Cover and leave to marinate in a cool place for up to 30 minutes but no longer as the cheese begins to toughen.

Fry the slices of baguette in olive oil until crisp and golden.

Drain the cheese mixture and arrange the cheese with its vegetable garnish on top of each slice.

BOTTOM LEFT TO RIGHT:
REBLOCHON AND RADISH CROÛTE
BRIOCHE CROÛTE WITH APRICOT
CHUTNEY AND GORGONZOLA
PROVENÇALE CROÛTE
ITALIAN CROSTINI
CHUTNEY CRUNCH

TOMATO AND BEANSPROUT CROÛTES

Soak beansprouts in cold water for 5 minutes before using. You'll be amazed at their crispness!

MAKES ABOUT 30

8 large slices of granary or rye bread
50g/2oz/¼ cup garlic butter (see page 137)
100g/4oz/1¼ cups Emmenthal cheese, grated
100g/4oz/¾ cup small beansprouts, chopped or
50g/2oz/¾ cup alfalfa sprouts
1 tablespoon freshly chopped parsley
1 teaspoon freshly chopped thyme
30-32 slices tomato, preferably plum tomatoes
salt and freshly milled pepper

Toast the bread slices lightly on both sides and spread with garlic butter.

Mix the cheese, beansprouts and herbs and season generously with salt and pepper.

Stamp out four rounds from each slice of toast about the same size as the tomato slices and place a slice of tomato on each one. Top with some of the cheese mixture and bake in a preheated oven at 220°C/425°F/gas mark 7 for about 4 minutes. Serve warm.

SCALLOP CROÛTES WITH SAUCE VIERGE

A sophisticated croûte with a lovely combination of scallops in a delicate olive oil dressing.

MAKES 10

10 thin slices of baguette
25g/1oz/2 tablespoons unsalted butter
20g/¾oz/4 teaspoons red (sweet) pepper fillet,
blanched, peeled and finely diced
15g/½oz/1 tablespoon green (sweet) pepper
fillet, blanched, peeled and finely diced
15g/½oz/3 teaspoons courgette (zucchini),
finely diced
5 fresh scallops, cut in half crossways
salt and freshly milled pepper
2 tablespoons olive oil
sauce vierge (see page 135)

Spread the slices of baguette with the butter and toast under a preheated grill until golden.

Mix the diced red and green pepper with the courgette and place some on each slice of baguette.

Dry the scallops on a kitchen cloth (dish towel) and season generously with salt and pepper. Heat the oil in a frying pan and very quickly fry the scallops on both sides until just sealed.

Place a scallop on top of each croûte and spoon a little sauce vierge on top.

ITALIAN CROSTINI

The original idea of this type of canapé was to use any little leftovers, such as ham or salami trimmings, combined with herbs, cheese, anchovies or other strongly flavoured foods. Make it quickly, heat it quickly and eat it at once – a delightful idea.

MAKES ABOUT 20

75g/3oz/6 tablespoons unsalted butter
120ml/4fl oz/½ cup olive oil
2 cloves of garlic, crushed
20 thin slices of baguette or small pieces
of ciabatta (Italian bread)
100g/4oz/½ cup Parma ham (prosciutto), diced
2 teaspoons freshly chopped sage
2 tablespoons freshly chopped parsley
100g/4oz Tallegio cheese, thinly sliced

Melt half the butter in a large frying pan, then add half the oil and one clove of the garlic. Turn ten of the baguette slices in the frying pan over a medium heat until crisp and golden. Remove from the pan and keep warm. Use the remaining butter, oil and garlic to fry the remaining bread slices. Add the ham to the frying pan and sauté quickly.

Remove from the heat and stir in the herbs. Spoon a little of the mixture on to each baguette slice.

Place a piece of cheese on each one and melt lightly under a preheated grill (broiler). Serve at once.

ALL RECIPES PHOTOGRAPHED ON PREVIOUS PAGE

CHUTNEY CRUNCHES

A personal version of the British 'left-overs' canapé.

MAKES 20

20 slices of baguette
garlic butter for spreading (see page 137)
20 teaspoons apricot chutney (see page 133)
225g/8oz goat's cheese
120ml/4fl oz/½ cup double (heavy) cream
20 tiny sprigs of chervil or parsley

Spread the slices of baguette with garlic butter and toast both sides.

Place a teaspoonful of chutney on each piece of bread. Cut the cheese in 20 even-sized pieces and place on top of the chutney.

Place the cream in a small saucepan and cook over a medium heat until reduced by half. Spoon a little over each croûte and brown quickly under a grill (broiler) preheated to its hottest setting.

Garnish each croûte with a sprig of chervil or parsley.

WARM GOAT'S CHEESE IN A SEED CRUST

Make absolutely sure that the cheese warms right to the middle, otherwise it leaves a very sharp taste.

MAKES 20

5 miniature Crottin Chauvignolles (or other goat's cheese)
400ml/14fl oz/1¾ cups olive oil
sprig of rosemary
sprig of lemon thyme
sprig of marjoram
2 cloves of garlic, sliced
1 egg, beaten
about 4 tablespoons poppy seeds
about 4 tablespoons sesame seeds
20 slices of baguette
garlic butter for spreading (see page 137)
40 leaves of corn salad (lamb's lettuce)
a little vinaigrette dressing

Cut each cheese in four slices and marinate in the oil with the herbs and garlic for at least 12 hours. It may be kept for several weeks in a sealed jar.

Remove the cheese from the oil and wipe off most of the oil with absorbent paper. Dip each piece of cheese in the beaten egg, then turn in the mixed poppy and sesame seeds until lightly coated. Place on a lightly oiled baking tray and bake in a preheated oven at 220°C/425°F/gas mark 7 for 2-3 minutes.

Spread the slices of baguette with garlic butter and toast lightly on both sides.

Moisten the corn salad with a little vinaigrette. Arrange four leaves of corn salad and a piece of cheese on each slice of toasted baguette. Serve warm.

PROVENÇALE CROÛTES

One of the modern versions of croûtes which favours the vegetarian. These seem to become more and more popular all the time – they are very light and digestible and when served warm with lots of herbs, have a delicious aroma.

Serve with full-bodied red wines.

MAKES 20

50ml/2fl oz/¼ cup olive oil
50g/2oz/⅓ cup onion, finely chopped
2 cloves of garlic, crushed
300g/10oz/1½ cups tomato fillets, diced
2 tablespoons freshly chopped oregano or marjoram
salt and pepper
20 slices of baguette
40g/1½oz/6 tablespoons Parmesan cheese, finely grated

Heat the oil and sweat the onion and garlic until translucent. Add the diced tomato and simmer for about 10 minutes until all the liquid has been absorbed. Add the oregano and season to taste.

Toast the slices of baguette lightly on both sides and spread with the tomato mixture. Sprinkle with the Parmesan cheese.

Place under a hot grill (broiler) and colour the cheese lightly. Serve warm.

ANCHOVY AND OLIVE CROUSTADES

MAKES 20

20g/³⁄₄oz/3-4 anchovy fillets, drained
a little milk
50g/2oz/3 tablespoons stoned (pitted)
green olives
20g/³⁄₄oz/2¹⁄₂ tablespoons shallot,
finely chopped
1 clove of garlic, crushed
2 tablespoons olive oil
20 slices of French bread, toasted
2 tablespoons freshly chopped sage
¹⁄₄ red (sweet) pepper, skinned and cut in fine
strips

Soak the anchovy in a little milk for 10 minutes. Drain thoroughly, then combine with the olives, shallot, garlic and olive oil in a food processor and work to a smooth paste.

Spread a generous amount on each slice of toast and top with freshly chopped sage and a little red pepper.

GARLIC AND HERB TOASTS

Lots of people avoid garlic, but contrary to many people's belief, once cooked it actually aids digestion and thins the blood, making it a valuable addition to the diet. Some cultures almost look upon it as a medicine.

MAKES 20

5 cloves of garlic, peeled
50ml/2fl oz/¹⁄₄ cup olive oil
1 fresh bay leaf
12 small sprigs of rosemary
5 large slices of brown bread
1 teaspoon freshly chopped chives
1 teaspoon freshly chopped marjoram
1 teaspoon freshly chopped sage
salt and freshly milled pepper

Just cover the garlic cloves with boiling water and boil for 30 seconds. Drain immediately.

Place the garlic in a jar with the olive oil, bay leaf and rosemary sprigs. Cover and leave in a cool place for at least 24 hours.

Toast the bread, then brush with the olive oil used in the marinade. Remove the crusts and cut each slice of bread in four triangles.

Remove the garlic and herbs from the oil. Thinly slice the garlic and finely chop the herbs. Mix all the herbs together.

Divide the garlic slices between the triangles of toast and sprinkle with the herbs. Season lightly with salt and generously with freshly milled pepper.

PHOTOGRAPH ON PAGE 106

LATKES

Latkes, a central European and Jewish speciality, are traditionally served with soured cream and apple sauce. They need to be very crisp and served almost straight away. Allow at least 3 per person as they seem to grow on you!

MAKES ABOUT 20

400g/14oz potatoes
1 tablespoon finely chopped onion
3 egg yolks
salt and freshly milled pepper
120ml/4fl oz/¹⁄₂ cup vegetable oil

Suggested toppings:
crème fraîche and chopped chives
crème fraîche and Keta caviar
soured cream and apple purée

Finely grate the potatoes and place in a kitchen cloth (dish towel). Squeeze out the water, then combine the grated potato with the onion and egg yolks and season generously with salt and pepper.

Heat the oil in a large frying pan. Place tablespoonfuls of the potato mixture in the pan and press each one to a thin cake. Fry for 8-10 minutes until golden brown on both sides. Drain on absorbent paper. Repeat until all the potato is used.

Serve the latkes topped with crème fraîche and chopped chives, crème fraîche and Keta caviar or soured cream and apple purée.

LATKES

CHICKEN LIVER CROÛTES

Again, one of the more modern croûton-style canapés adapted from Italian peasant cooking.

MAKES ABOUT 20

50g/2oz/¼ cup unsalted butter
6 tablespoons olive oil
20 tiny slices of ciabbata or other Italian bread
25g/1oz/3 tablespoons onion, chopped
1 clove of garlic, crushed
225g/8oz/1 cup chicken livers, cleaned and chopped
20g/¾oz/1⅓ tablespoons capers, chopped
2 anchovy fillets, chopped
1½ teaspoons freshly chopped oregano
1 teaspoon fresh lime juice
salt and freshly milled pepper

Heat the butter and 4 tablespoons of the oil in a frying pan and fry the slices of bread in batches until crisp and golden on both sides. Keep warm.

Heat the remaining oil and sweat the onion and garlic until translucent. Add the chicken livers and cook quickly until browned on all sides. Stir in the capers, anchovy fillets, oregano and lime juice. Season to taste.

Pile the mixture on the fried bread slices and serve warm.

PLANTAIN CRISPS

Jamaica is the home of the plantain crisp where they are usually served alongside ovenbaked shavings of fresh coconut with what else but a Rum punch!

Plantain skins naturally turn from green to yellow to brown. Choose them when the skin is yellow-brown.

4 medium-ripe plantains, peeled
oil for deep frying
salt

Using a mandolin or very sharp knife, cut the plantains in wafer-thin slices.

Heat the oil and fry the plantain slices in batches until crisp and golden. Drain on absorbent paper.

Sprinkle with salt and toss well. Serve warm or cold.

GARLIC SABLES

MAKES ABOUT 40

½ quantity shortcrust pastry (see page 138)
3 cloves of garlic, finely chopped
beaten egg to glaze

On a lightly floured surface, roll out the pastry and sprinkle with the garlic. Fold and roll the pastry until the garlic is evenly distributed. Roll out the pastry thinly and stamp out 4cm/1½ inch rounds using a serrated cutter.

Place on a lightly buttered baking tray and brush with beaten egg. Leave to rest in a cool place for at least 20 minutes.

Bake in a preheated oven at 200°C/400°F/gas mark 6 for about 15 minutes until golden. Serve warm.

SMOKED CHICKEN AND AVOCADO ON PUMPERNICKEL CRUSTS

MAKES ABOUT 30

½ smoked chicken
2 small ripe avocados
50ml/2fl oz/¼ cup dressing
8 slices of pumpernickle
50ml/2fl oz/¼ cup olive oil
1 clove of garlic, crushed
salt
a few Webb's (leaf) lettuce leaves, washed

Remove the chicken meat from the bone and discard the skin. Cut in small dice. Halve, peel and stone (pit) the avocados and cut in similar-sized dice. Combine the chicken and avocado with the dressing.

Cut each slice of pumpernickel in four squares. Heat the olive oil in a frying pan and add the garlic. Toss the bread lightly in the oil and sprinkle with salt. Cook until crisp, then drain on absorbent kitchen paper.

Place a small piece of lettuce on each pumpernickel square, then arrange a little chicken and avocado mixture on top.

ANCHOVY STICKS

Marinated anchovy fillets make a good alternative to those canned in oil.

MAKES 20

200g/7oz puff pastry
1 egg, beaten
20 anchovy fillets
½ red pepper, blanched, seeds removed and skinned
½ green pepper, blanched, seeds removed and skinned

On a lightly floured surface, roll out the pastry about 18cm/7 inch wide and brush with beaten egg to glaze. Arrange the anchovy fillets about 9mm/⅜ inch apart and 2cm/¾ inch from the top of the pastry. Fold over the top of the pastry by 9mm/⅛ inch and the bottom of the pastry by about 6cm/2½ inch. Press the pastry down with the back of a knife between each anchovy fillet and brush with beaten egg.

Cut each pepper in 40 fine strips and arrange two of each colour over the anchovy fillets. Leave to rest in a cool place for at least 20 minutes

Place on a lightly greased baking tray (sheet) and bake in the oven at 220°C/425°F/gas mark 7 for 12–15 minutes until crisp and golden. Cut in sticks with a sharp knife and serve warm.

RILLETTE ON GARLIC CROÛTES

Traditional French peasant food turned into a canapé – it needs to be very well seasoned to maximise flavour.

MAKES ABOUT 50

25g/1oz/2 tablespoons unsalted butter
25g/1oz/3 tablespoons shallots, finely chopped
1 clove of garlic, crushed
100g/4oz/½ cup raw ham, diced
100g/4oz/½ cup shoulder pork, diced
25g/1oz/1-2 slices streaky bacon, diced
¼ teaspoon each freshly chopped sage, rosemary and thyme
50ml/2fl oz/¼ cup dry white wine
pinch of freshly grated nutmeg
120ml/4fl oz/½ cup chicken stock
freshly milled pepper
2 egg yolks
50ml/2fl oz/¼ cup double (heavy) cream
15g/½oz/1 tablespoon gherkins, finely chopped
about 50 thin slices French bread
garlic butter (see page 137)
salad leaves and gherkins to garnish

Melt the butter and sauté the shallots and garlic until translucent. Add the meats and cook for 5 minutes, allowing the meat to colour slightly. Add the herbs and deglaze the pan with white wine. Add the nutmeg and chicken stock. Season generously with pepper. Cover and simmer over the gentlest heat for 1 hour until the meats are tender and just moist.

Remove the pan from the heat, add the egg yolks and cream and work in a food processor to a coarse paste. Add the gherkins and chill the rillette mixture until required.

Spread each slice of bread with a little garlic butter and toast until golden. Spread a little of the rillette mixture on to each croûte and garnish with salad leaves and gherkins.

ONIONS AND NUTS

A very unusual mixture you might say, but the result is one of sweetness from the onions mixed with a slight bitterness from the nuts.

They may be served warm or cold and are delicious alongside a selection of cheese. Serve with full-bodied fruity wines from the Moselle and Alsace regions.

50ml/2fl oz/¼ cup dry white wine
50g/2oz/3½ tablespoons brown sugar
400g/14oz small button onions, peeled
200ml/7fl oz/scant 1 cup sauce Provençale (see page 133)
200g/7oz/2 cups walnut halves, toasted

Place the white wine and sugar in a saucepan and bring to the boil. Add the onions and cook over a very gentle heat for about 10 minutes until the wine has evaporated and the onions are just tender and caramelised. Add the sauce Provençale and walnuts and simmer gently until heated through.

Serve the onions and walnuts speared with cocktail sticks (toothpicks).

PETITS FOURS FRUIT TARTLETS

S U G A R

A N D

Spice

Although many claim to be on a diet, the dessert stage in any meal forms a very important part of most people's eating habits, and so it should! You will always find guests looking forward to a little sweetmeat with coffee to round off their meal even if they have not indulged in puddings.

The key point is the intensity of flavours and tastes such as ginger, lemon, chocolate, coffee and maple syrup. These ingredients feature strongly, served in feather-light shells of crisp rich pastry, filo pastry or even tuiles.

The traditional has not to be ignored either – try miniature syrup tarts, a gift of the Gods!

Health is given a little consideration with fresh fruits and fruit dips used effectively in colourful arrangements – they could even be used as decorations in place of flowers.

For the grande finale, what could be more impressive than the Black and White Chocolate Pralines – smoke rising from dry ice (perhaps even in different colours for one-upmanship) as you present miniature ice creams wrapped in chocolate.

Here are two fruit-based cocktails ideal
to serve with sweet frivolities, specially
created by Peter Dorelli, Head Barman at
The Savoy.

PLYMOUTH PEAK

¼ gin
¼ cranberry juice
¼ passion fruit nectar
¼ lime juice
egg white

Shake and decorate with a cherry and a
slice of lime.

NOT TONIGHT

¼ vodka
¼ Mandarine Napoleon
½ pineapple juice
coconut cream

Blend with ice and decorate with a
wedge of fresh pineapple and a cherry.

STRAWBERRY TARTLETS/ PETITS FOURS FRUIT TARTLETS

A simple but spectacular combination. Replace the strawberries with any prepared fruit of your choice and arrange attractively in the pastry cases. Brush with apricot glaze. Add a tiny sprig of mint and dust with icing sugar if wished.

MAKES ABOUT 20

175 g/6oz nut pastry or sweet pastry (see page 138)
75g/3oz/6 tablespoons Mascarpone cheese
150g/5oz/1¼ cups strawberries
2 tablespoons redcurrant jelly or seedless raspberry jam

Press a small piece of pastry into each 5cm/2 inch tartlet tin (pan) so that it covers the tin evenly. Trim the edges to neaten them and prick the base of each one with a fork. Chill the pastry for at least 20 minutes.

Place the tartlet tins on a baking tray and bake in a preheated oven at 190°C/375°F/gas mark 5 for 20 minutes until golden brown. Leave to cool, then remove from the tins.

Spoon a tiny amount of Mascarpone cheese into each tartlet case.

Finely chop the strawberries. Warm the redcurrant jelly or raspberry jam and stir in the fruit. Leave to cool, then spoon a little into each pastry case.

PHOTOGRAPH ON PAGE 114

LOGANBERRY PALMIERS

Loganberries make this a seasonal item. You can replace the Scottish berries with raspberries or blackberries.

MAKES 20

200g/7oz puff pastry
sugar syrup (see page 137)
50g/2oz/¼ cup caster (superfine) sugar
100ml/3½fl oz/scant ½ cup pastry cream (see page 137)
50ml/2fl oz/¼ cup double (heavy) cream, whipped
40 loganberries

On a lightly floured surface, roll out the puff pastry to a rectangle measuring 30 × 18cm/12 × 7 inches, then cut in half to make two rectangles measuring 18 × 15cm/7 × 6 inches. Brush each piece of pastry with sugar syrup, then sprinkle with half the sugar. Fold the short sides of each rectangle in to meet in the centre, brush with sugar syrup and sprinkle with half the remaining sugar. Fold over and press down gently. Leave to rest in the refrigerator for at least 20 minutes.

Cut each length of pastry in 20 slices. Place the pastry slices on a lightly buttered baking tray and sprinkle with the remaining sugar. Bake in a preheated oven at 220°C/425°F/ gas mark 7 for 10 minutes, turning the palmiers over after the first 5 minutes, until crisp and golden. Cool on a wire tray.

Mix the pastry cream and whipped cream together and using a piping bag fitted with a small star nozzle (tube), pipe a rosette of cream on to half the palmiers. Top each one with two loganberries and a plain palmier.

MARINATED STRAWBERRIES

Created originally as a Wimbledon cocktail, this has been served ever since because of its popularity. The flavour of Pernod or anise is surprisingly spectacular with juicy ripe strawberries.

MAKES ABOUT 30

450g/1lb medium-sized ripe strawberries
6 tablespoons Pernod or anise
150ml/¼ pint/⅔ cup double (heavy) cream
2 tablespoons icing (confectioners') sugar, sifted
1 teaspoon green peppercorns, finely crushed
25 g/1oz/2½ tablespoons flaked almonds, toasted

Wash, then hull the strawberries. Place in a bowl and pour the Pernod or anise over the fruit. Leave to marinate in the refrigerator for 10 minutes. Drain the strawberries and reserve the juice.

Lightly whip the cream and icing sugar, then add 2 tablespoons of the reserved juice and the peppercorns and whip until thick. Add more juice if a stronger flavour is preferred. Stir in the flaked almonds.

Arrange the strawberries on a serving plate. Press a cocktail stick (toothpick) into each one. Spoon the cream into a bowl and serve with the strawberries for dipping.

SCONES WITH EXOTIC FRUIT

These colourful scones are always popular – who could resist the mix of clotted cream, summer berries and mint?

MAKES ABOUT 20

200g/7oz/1²⁄₃ cups plain (all-purpose) flour
1 tablespoon baking powder
50g/2oz/¹⁄₄ cup unsalted butter
50g/2oz/¹⁄₄ cup caster (superfine) sugar
25g/1oz/2 tablespoons sultanas
6-7 tablespoons milk
beaten egg to glaze
clotted cream
an assortment of summer berries, kiwi fruit,
papaya and mango
sprigs of fresh mint
icing (confectioners') sugar

Sift the flour and baking powder together. Rub in the butter until the mixture resembles fine crumbs, then stir in the sugar and sultanas. Add sufficient milk to the dry ingredients to give a firm manageable dough.

On a lightly floured surface, roll out the dough 2cm/¾ inch thick and stamp out 4-5cm/1½-2 inch rounds. Place on a lightly buttered baking tray and brush with beaten egg to glaze. Bake in a preheated oven at 220°C/425°F/gas mark 7 for about 15 minutes until risen and golden. Cool on a wire tray.

Cut the scones in half, top generously with clotted cream and arrange the fruit attractively on top. Decorate each one with a sprig of mint and dust with icing sugar.

TOFFEE TARTLETS

MAKES ABOUT 20

For the pastry:
125g/4¹⁄₂oz/heaped 1 cup plain
(all-purpose) flour
50g/2oz/4¹⁄₂ tablespoons icing
(confectioners') sugar
50g/2oz/¹⁄₄ cup unsalted butter
2 tablespoons beaten egg
finely grated rind of ¹⁄₂ orange
icing (confectioners') sugar to dust

For the filling:
25g/1oz/3 tablespoons pine kernels
25g/1oz/2¹⁄₂ tablespoons flaked almonds
50g/2oz/¹⁄₄ cup golden (light corn) syrup
50g/2oz/¹⁄₄ cup caster (superfine) sugar
50g/2oz/¹⁄₄ cup unsalted butter
25g/1oz/¹⁄₄ cup sultanas
25g/1oz/2 tablespoons glacé (candied)
cherries, chopped
25g/1oz/2 tablespoons citron peel, chopped

For the pastry, sift the flour and icing sugar into a bowl. Rub in the butter until the mixture resembles fine crumbs, then stir in the egg and orange rind and work together to form a firm dough.

On a lightly floured surface, roll out the pastry and use to line about 20 4cm/1½ inch tartlet tins (pans). Leave to rest in a cool place for at least 20 minutes. Bake blind in a preheated oven at 190°C/375°F/gas mark 5 for 20 minutes.

For the filling, toast the nuts for 8-10 minutes until golden. Melt the golden syrup, caster sugar and butter in a saucepan. Bring slowly to the boil and boil for about 2 minutes until a light toffee colour. Stir in the fruit, peel and nuts. Dust the cooled pastry cases with icing sugar, spoon in the filling and leave to set.

FRESH GINGER HORNS

MAKES ABOUT 30

50g/2oz/¹⁄₄ cup unsalted butter
50g/2oz/¹⁄₄ cup caster (superfine) sugar
50g/2oz/¹⁄₄ cup golden (light corn) syrup
50g/2oz/5 tablespoons plain (all-purpose)
flour, sifted
2 teaspoons freshly grated root ginger
whipped cream
small pieces of stem ginger or marron glacé
to decorate

Place the butter, sugar and golden syrup in a saucepan and heat gently until the butter melts. Stir in the flour and ginger.

Spoon six ¾-teaspoon quantities of the mixture on to a baking tray and bake in a preheated oven at 180°C/350°F/gas mark 4 for about 5 minutes until golden brown.

Allow to cool slightly, then remove from the tray and immediately wrap each one around a cream horn tin (mould). Leave to become cold, then remove from the tin. If the biscuits harden too quickly, they may be returned to the oven to soften.

Use all the mixture to make more ginger horns.

Using a piping bag fitted with a star nozzle (tube), pipe a little whipped cream into each horn and decorate with a piece of stem ginger or marron glacé.

TOFFEE TARTLETS
FRESH GINGER HORNS
SCONES WITH EXOTIC FRUIT

HAZELNUT MACAROONS

Excellent with port or brandy!

MAKES ABOUT 30

2 egg whites
pinch of salt
175g/6oz/¾ cup caster (superfine) sugar
50g/2oz/¼ cup skinned hazelnuts, roasted
and ground
50g/2oz/¼ cup ground almonds
2 tablespoons finely chopped hazelnuts
or almonds
whipped cream

Whisk the egg whites with a pinch of salt until stiff, then whisk in the sugar a spoonful at a time until the mixture is thick and glossy. Fold in the ground hazelnuts and almonds.

Use the mixture to fill a piping bag fitted with a 2cm/¾ inch plain nozzle (tube) and pipe about 60 small drops on baking trays lined with baking parchment. Sprinkle half of them with chopped nuts. Bake in a preheated oven at 180°C/350°F/gas mark 4 for 15-20 minutes until golden brown. Leave to cool on a wire tray.

Sandwich the macaroons together with a little whipped cream, using the nut-sprinkled macaroons for the tops.

HORNS OF PLENTY

MAKES ABOUT 20

200g/7oz puff pastry
egg white
caster (superfine) sugar
50g/2oz/2 squares luxury plain (semi-sweet)
chocolate, melted
50g/2oz/3½ tablespoons mango, puréed
200ml/7fl oz/scant 1 cup double (heavy) cream,
whipped, or half cream and half pastry cream
(see page 137)
finely diced mango or finely chopped pistachio
nuts to decorate

On a lightly floured surface roll out the pastry about 3mm/⅛ inch thick. Cut out strips of pastry measuring about 18 × 1.5cm/7 × ½ inches and brush lightly with egg white.

Butter cream horn tins and carefully wrap a strip of pastry around each one, starting at the point and overlapping slightly on each turn of the pastry. Sprinkle each pastry horn with caster sugar. Leave to rest for at least 20 minutes in a cool place.

Place the pastry horns on a lightly buttered baking tray and bake in a preheated oven at 220°C/425°F/gas mark 7 for 10-15 minutes until lightly golden. Leave to cool, then carefully twist the pastry off the metal tins.

Dip the open ends of the horns in melted chocolate and leave to set.

Mix together the mango purée and cream and using a piping bag fitted with a small star nozzle (tube), pipe a whirl of cream into each horn. Top each with a little finely diced mango or a sprinkling of pistachio nuts.

FILO TULIPS WITH GREEK YOGHURT AND YELLOW FRUITS

The versatility of filo pastry is virtually endless – here frilly little pastry cases are filled with greek yoghurt and fresh fruits, so they should be eaten fairly quickly once filled.

MAKES ABOUT 20

8 large sheets of filo pastry
50g/2oz/¼ cup unsalted butter, melted
8 tablespoons strained Greek yoghurt
175g/6oz/1¼ cups prepared yellow fruits such
as apricot, peach, nectarine or mango, cut in
small dice
icing (confectioners') sugar

Lay out one sheet of filo pastry and brush with a little melted butter. Lay three more sheets on top, brushing a little butter between each one.

Cut about ten 9cm/3½ inch squares from the filo pastry and press each one into a 5cm/2 inch tartlet tin (pan).

Repeat with the remaining four sheets of pastry.

Bake the filo pastry cases in a preheated oven at 190°C/375°F/gas mark 5 for 10-12 minutes until golden brown. Leave to cool, then remove from the tins.

When completely cold, spoon a little yoghurt into each filo pastry tulip and top with some diced fruit. Sprinkle with a generous dusting of icing sugar and serve at once.

COCONUT SAMOSAS

Here are samosas with a difference and although their ingredients may seem slightly strange, they form a very harmonious and delightful dish – you'll be surprised!

MAKES 20

5 tablespoons milk
50g/2oz/¼ cup caster (superfine) sugar
50g/2oz/½ cup desiccated coconut
50g/2oz/¼ cup sultanas, roughly chopped
½ teaspoon finely crushed cardamom seeds
2½ large sheets of filo pastry
40g/1½oz/3 tablespoons unsalted butter, melted

Place the milk, sugar and coconut in a saucepan and cook over a gentle heat until all the liquid has been absorbed. Add the sultanas and cardamom seeds and leave to become cold.

Cut each sheet of filo in eight strips about 5cm/2 inches wide and brush each one with melted butter. Place a teaspoonful of the coconut filling at one end of each strip, then fold the pastry over the filling to make a triangular shape. Continue rolling and folding the pastry over to form a small triangular parcel.

Place on a baking tray, brush with the remaining melted butter and bake in a preheated oven at 190°C/375°F/gas mark 5 for 10-12 minutes until crisp and golden. Serve warm.

GRAPE SHORTCAKES WITH ALMONDS

These little shortcakes are very popular in the south of France, and are delicious with a glass of Champagne or sparkling dessert wine.

MAKES 20

For the shortcakes:
75g/3oz/½ cup plain (all-purpose) flour, sifted
pinch of salt
50g/2oz/¼ cup unsalted butter, softened
25g/1oz/2 tablespoons caster (superfine) sugar
plus extra for sprinkling
½ tablespoon beaten egg

For the pastry cream and topping:
1 egg yolk
25g/1oz/2 tablespoons caster (superfine) sugar
1 tablespoon cornflour (cornstarch)
1 tablespoon plain (all-purpose) flour
150ml/¼ pint/⅔ cup milk
50ml/2fl oz/¼ cup strained natural yoghurt
10 black grapes, halved and seeds removed
10 white grapes, halved and seeds removed
1 tablespoon nibbed almonds, roasted

Sift the flour and salt into a bowl and rub in the butter until the mixture resembles fine crumbs. Stir in the sugar and beaten egg and work together to form a firm, manageable dough.

On a lightly floured surface, roll out the dough about 5mm/¼ inch thick and stamp out 4cm/1½ inch rounds. Place the rounds on a lightly buttered baking tray and sprinkle with caster sugar. Leave to rest in a cool place for at least 20 minutes. Prick with a fork and bake in a preheated oven at 180°C/350°F/gas mark 4 for 10-12 minutes until golden. Cool on a wire tray.

For the pastry cream, mix the egg yolk, sugar and flours with a little of the milk to make a smooth paste. Heat the remaining milk and stir into the egg mixture. Return to the saucepan and cook, stirring until thickened.

Transfer the pastry cream to a bowl and beat with a hand-held electric mixer until cool. Leave to become cold, then beat in the yoghurt.

Using a piping bag fitted with a large star nozzle (tube), pipe a rosette of pastry cream on each shortcake and top with a black and a white grape half. Sprinkle with the nibbed almonds.

APPLE AND RUM FRANGIPANE TARTS

Frangipane is a flavour from the 'gourmet heaven' – however it is used.

MAKES ABOUT 20

175g/6oz sweet pastry (see page 138)

For the apple purée:
*1½ dessert apples such as Cox's orange pippin
or Jonas gold
1½ tablespoons water
1½ tablespoons caster (superfine) sugar*

For the rum frangipane:
*50g/2oz/¼ cup caster (superfine) sugar
50g/2oz/⅓ cup ground almonds
25g/1oz/2 tablespoons unsalted butter, melted
and cooled
1 egg yolk
1 tablespoon dark rum
finely chopped angelica or candied fruit
to decorate*

On a lightly floured surface, roll out the pastry thinly and use to line about 20 tiny 1 tablespoon capacity tartlet tins (pans). Chill until required.

Peel, core and chop the apples and simmer gently with the water and sugar for 12–15 minutes to make a thick purée. Leave to go cold.

Beat together all the ingredients for the frangipane.

Spoon about ½ teaspoon apple purée and 1 teaspoon frangipane into each pastry case. Sprinkle with a little angelica and bake in a preheated oven at 190°C/ 375°F/gas mark 5 for about 20 minutes until golden.

Cool slightly, then remove from the tins. Serve warm.

BLACK AND WHITE CHOCOLATE PRALINES

These pralines were created some seven years ago for the marriage of an old client of The Savoy who wanted something spectacular to surprise the rather beautiful young lady he was to marry. It was so effective that it has now become a tradition to serve them with the compliments of management and kitchen alike at virtually every wedding reception in the hotel.

It is essential to have dry ice to prepare this recipe. The tiny balls of ice cream must be hardened on a metal tray set on dry ice. This makes them cold enough to be dipped in the chocolate which is at room temperature. Check with a local ice supplier for dry ice.

The pralines can be made a few days in advance, stored in the freezer and brought out to serve as the highlight and finale to your party.

MAKES ABOUT 20

*a small amount of dry ice
100g/4oz/½ cup ice cream of your choice
100g/4oz/4 squares luxury white chocolate
100g/4oz/4 squares luxury plain
(semisweet) chocolate
120ml/4fl oz/½ cup double (heavy) cream*

Place a metal tray over the dry ice. Using a small melon ball scoop (parisian scoop), shape small balls of ice cream and place on the tray to harden. Stick a cocktail stick into each one before it hardens.

Chop the white chocolate and place in a small bowl with 4 tablespoons of the cream. Chop the plain chocolate and place in a small bowl with the remaining cream. Melt both chocolates over a saucepan of simmering water and stir until smooth.

Dip half the ice cream balls in the dark chocolate mixture one at a time and return to the metal tray immediately to harden. Repeat with the white chocolate. Store the ice cream balls in the freezer in a rigid container until required.

For a dramatic presentation place a small amount of dry ice in a bowl and pour a little boiling water on to the ice. This forms a 'mist'. Set the pralines on a plate and place on the bowl of dry ice. Serve immediately.

BLACK AND WHITE CHOCOLATE PRALINES

RENDEZVOUS OF FRUITS WITH FRUIT COULIS

You can make a wonderful centrepiece with this dish – almost a fruit buffet to decorate the table. Whole fruits and prepared fruits can be attractively displayed together letting your imagination run wild with the seasonal and the exotic.

Choose from a selection of the following fruits and prepare in bite-sized pieces according to shape and size:
Melon (honeydew, Ogen, Charentais and watermelon), pineapple, kiwi, papaya, mango, lychees, figs, Cape gooseberries (physalis), cherries, banana, pear, strawberries, star fruit, nectarines and peaches, summer berries.

RASPBERRY COULIS

300g/10oz/2 cups raspberries
2 teaspoons lemon juice
40g/1½oz/3 tablespoons icing
(confectioners') sugar

Liquidise (blend) all the ingredients and pass through a fine sieve.

GOOSEBERRY COULIS

450g/1lb dessert gooseberries
120ml/4fl oz/½ cup sugar syrup (see page 137)
2 teaspoons lemon juice

Simmer the gooseberries in the sugar syrup and lemon juice until just tender. Purée in a liquidiser or pass through a mouli, then through a fine sieve. Cool and add extra syrup to taste, if wished.

ANISEED COOKIES WITH STRAWBERRY

Aniseed is underused in our cooking in this country, not only in desserts, but also in fish sauces and salads. These cookies might convince the non-believers!

Bake the mixture in small batches so that there is plenty of time to shape these tiny biscuits before they cool and become crisp. They can be made in advance and stored in an airtight tin.

MAKES ABOUT 40

2 egg whites
pinch of salt
pinch of cream of tartar
65g/2½oz/5 tablespoons caster (superfine) sugar
1 large egg yolk
65g/2½oz/5 tablespoons plain (all-purpose) flour, sifted
65g/2½oz/5 tablespoons unsalted butter, melted and cooled
1 teaspoon ground aniseed
whipped cream and strawberries to decorate

Whisk the egg whites with a pinch of salt and a pinch of cream of tartar until the mixture has a soft peak consistency. Whisk in the sugar a little at a time until the mixture is very stiff.

Mix the egg yolk, flour, butter and aniseed together, then add the egg white and beat until smooth.

Line baking trays with baking parchment or rice paper. Drop teaspoonfuls of the mixture on to the trays and spread out evenly to make 4cm/1½ inch diameter rounds.

Bake in a preheated oven at 220°C/425°F/gas mark 7 for 6-7 minutes until golden brown. Immediately lay the biscuits over a thin rolling pin or lengths of wooden dowelling to shape them. Leave to cool and harden.

Using a piping bag fitted with a star nozzle (tube), pipe a little whipped cream into each cookie and top with a small piece of strawberry or a wild strawberry.

HONEY MADELEINES

MAKES ABOUT 40

2 eggs
75g/3oz/6 tablespoons caster (superfine) sugar
15g/½oz/1 tablespoon soft brown sugar
90g/3½oz/¾ cup plain (all-purpose) flour
1 teaspoon baking powder
pinch of salt
15g/½oz/1 tablespoon honey
90g/3½oz/7 tablespoons unsalted butter, melted

Beat the eggs and sugars together until thick and pale. Sift the flour, baking powder and salt together and add to the egg mixture. Beat in the honey and butter until evenly combined.

Spoon the mixture into buttered madeleine moulds (narrow shell-shaped pans) and bake in a preheated oven at 190°C/375°F/gas mark 5 for 10-15 minutes until risen and golden brown.

Cool slightly, then unmould. Serve fresh.

MINIATURE SYRUP TARTS

Golden syrup is the traditional ingredient of our syrup tarts whilst across the Atlantic they favour maple syrup – whichever you use they are unforgettable.

MAKES ABOUT 30

200g/7oz sweet pastry (see page 138)
175g/6oz/1 cup maple syrup or golden (light corn) syrup
25g/1oz/3 tablespoons ground almonds
½ teaspoon finely grated lemon rind
2 teaspoons lemon juice
1½ tablespoons beaten egg
3 tablespoons double (heavy) cream
40g/1½oz/¾ cup fresh breadcrumbs

On a lightly floured surface, roll out the pastry thinly and use to line about 30 tiny (1 tablespoon capacity) tartlet tins (pans). Chill until required.

Combine all the ingredients for the filling and spoon about 1 teaspoonful of mixture into each pastry case.

Bake in a preheated oven at 190°C/375°F/gas mark 5 for 15-20 minutes until just set and golden brown. Allow to cool slightly, then remove from the tins and serve just warm.

RICH CHOCOLATE SQUARES

Rich they are, but if you're 'into' chocolate you'll love them!

MAKES ABOUT 30

2 large eggs, separated
75g/3oz/6 tablespoons caster (superfine) sugar
½ teaspoon vanilla extract
100g/4oz/4 squares luxury plain (semisweet) chocolate, melted
50g/2oz/⅓ cup ground almonds
40g/1½oz/¼ cup plain (all-purpose) flour
½ teaspoon baking powder
100g/4oz/½ cup unsalted butter
pinch of salt
icing (confectioners') sugar to dust

Lightly butter and line the base of a 20cm/8 inch square cake tin (pan), with greaseproof (wax) paper or baking parchment.

Whisk the egg yolks, sugar and vanilla extract until smooth and pale. Stir in the melted chocolate, ground almonds and flour sifted together with the baking powder. Melt the butter and stir into the chocolate mixture.

Whisk the egg whites with a pinch of salt until stiff, then fold into the chocolate mixture until evenly combined. Transfer to the prepared tin. Bake in a preheated oven at 180°C/350°F/gas mark 4 for 20-25 minutes until firm to the touch.

Cool in the tin, then transfer to a cooling tray and leave to become cold. Dust with icing (confectioners') sugar and cut in small squares.

CAPE GOOSEBERRIES IN CARAMEL

Cape gooseberries, also known as physalis, originated as the name suggests in South Africa. This delightful small yellow fruit is encased in a paper-like shroud which is peeled back to reveal the fruit. Its flavour is sharp but sweet and leaves a lingering taste of lemon and almond in the mouth. Dipping in caramel or in fondant can bring out the best of its flavour.

MAKES 20

20 Cape gooseberries
225g/8oz/1 cup caster (superfine) sugar
generous pinch of cream of tartar
2 tablespoons water

Peel back the lantern-shaped cover from each Cape gooseberry and twist it where it joins the fruit. Wipe the fruit if it is sticky but ensure that it is dry before dipping in the caramel.

Place the sugar in a saucepan. Add the cream of tartar mixed with the water and heat gently until the sugar dissolves. Use a pastry brush dipped in cold water to brush off any sugar which may crystallise around the sides of the saucepan whilst the caramel is being prepared. Bring to the boil and boil to a medium caramel colour.

Place the saucepan immediately in a bowl of cold water to prevent the caramel becoming darker, and quickly dip each Cape gooseberry in the caramel.

Place on a sheet of baking parchment or a buttered tray until the caramel sets.

PHOTOGRAPH ON PAGE 127

MINIATURE CHRISTMAS PUDDINGS

MAKES ABOUT 30

For the pastry:
100g/4oz/½ cup unsalted butter
175g/6oz/1⅓ cups plain (all-purpose) flour
25g/1oz/2 tablespoons caster (superfine) sugar
1 tablespoon cold water
icing (confectioners') sugar

For the filling:
450g/1lb/2½ cups rich fruit cake, crumbled
3 tablespoons apricot jam
3 tablespoons dark rum
royal icing (white frosting)
marzipan (almond paste)
edible red and green colourings

For the pastry, rub the butter into the flour, then add the sugar and mix to a firm dough with the water.

Roll out the pastry on a lightly floured surface and use to line about 30 5cm/2 inch tartlet tins (pans). Leave to rest in a cool place for at least 20 minutes. Bake blind in a preheated oven at 190°C/375°F/gas mark 5 for 20 minutes. Cool and dust with icing sugar.

For the filling, combine the fruit cake crumbs, apricot jam and rum until evenly mixed, then shape into about 30 balls.

Place a ball in each pastry case. Drizzle a tiny amount of royal icing on each ball to represent the sauce on the pudding. Leave to set.

Colour a little marzipan green and shape about 60 green leaves. Colour a little marzipan red and shape about 90 berries. Position three berries and two leaves on each pudding.

LEMON FEUILLETÉS

In this recipe the sharpness of the lemon contrasts beautifully with the bitter chocolate and delicate sponge.

MAKES ABOUT 50

For the sponge:
2 eggs
50g/2oz/¼ cup caster (superfine) sugar
40g/1½oz/¼ cup plain (all-purpose) flour, sifted

For the topping:
3 egg yolks
2 egg whites
finely grated rind of 2 lemons
120ml/4fl oz/½ cup fresh lemon juice, strained
125g/4½oz/9 tablespoons caster (superfine) sugar
100g/4oz/½ cup unsalted butter
2 teaspoons gelatine
2 tablespoons dry white wine
100g/4oz/4 squares luxury plain (semisweet) chocolate

Lightly grease and line a 33 × 23cm/13 × 9 inch Swiss (jelly) roll tin (pan) with greaseproof (wax) paper.

Whisk the eggs and sugar together with an electric whisk until the mixture is thick and pale. The beaters should leave a strong trail in the mixture.

Fold in the flour and transfer the mixture to the prepared tin. Level the surface and bake in a preheated oven at 220°C/425°F/gas mark 7 for about 10 minutes until risen and firm to the touch. Cool on a wire tray, then peel off the lining paper.

For the topping, whisk the egg yolks, egg whites, lemon rind and juice, and sugar together. Then cook in a double boiler or a basin set over simmering water for 30-40 minutes until thickened, stirring frequently. Melt 65g/2½oz/heaped ¼ cup of the butter and stir into the lemon mixture.

Dissolve the gelatine in the white wine over a gentle heat, then stir in a little of the lemon mixture and return to the bulk of the mixture.

Trim the edges from the sponge and transfer to a lightly oiled 30 × 20cm/12 × 8 inch shallow tin. Spoon the lemon mixture on top and level the surface. Chill for about 4 hours until set.

Melt the chocolate with the remaining butter, spread over the lemon mixture and chill until set. Cut in small pieces.

MINIATURE CHRISTMAS PUDDINGS
CAPE GOOSEBERRIES IN CARAMEL
LEMON FEUILLETÉS

FLORENTINES

The florentines may be neatened to a perfect round with a cutter whilst still warm.

MAKES ABOUT 30

50g/2oz/¼ cup unsalted butter
50g/2oz/¼ cup caster (superfine) sugar
25g/1oz/3 tablespoons pistachio nuts, chopped
25g/1oz/3 tablespoons walnuts, chopped
25g/1oz/2½ tablespoons flaked almonds
50g/2oz/⅓ cup candied peel, chopped
50g/2oz/⅓ cup glacé (candied)
cherries, chopped
1 tablespoon double (heavy) cream
75g/3oz/3 squares luxury plain (semisweet)
chocolate, melted
75g/3oz/3 squares milk or white
chocolate, melted

Melt the butter in a small saucepan. Add the sugar, bring to a fast boil then remove from the heat. Stir in the remaining ingredients.

Line baking trays with baking parchment and drop one teaspoonful quantities of the mixture at intervals on the trays. Bake in a preheated oven at 190°C/375°F/gas mark 5 for 5-6 minutes until golden brown. Leave to become cold on the trays.

Spread a little chocolate on the back of each florentine and leave to set.

WARM CHEESECAKE TRIANGLES

These must be served just warm to bring out the very best of their flavour.

MAKES 30

For the pastry:
100g/4oz/½ cup unsalted butter
50g/2oz/¼ cup caster (superfine) sugar
pinch of salt
2 tablespoons beaten egg
175g/6oz/1⅓ cups plain (all-purpose)
flour, sifted

For the filling:
100g/4oz/½ cup medium-fat soft cheese
50g/2oz/¼ cup caster (superfine) sugar
few drops of vanilla extract
pinch of salt
1 tablespoon cornflour (cornstarch)
2 egg yolks
100ml/3½fl oz/scant ½ cup double (heavy)
cream
finely grated rind of 1 lemon
juice of ½ lemon
1 egg white
icing (confectioners') sugar to dust

Cream the butter and sugar together, then add a pinch of salt and the beaten egg. Fold in the flour to give a soft paste. Chill for at least 1 hour.

On a lightly floured surface, roll out about one-fifth of the pastry and use to line a 10cm/4 inch flan tin (tartpan). Trim the edges of the pastry. Line four more flan tins in the same way. Chill until required.

For the filling, mix the soft cheese, caster sugar, vanilla extract, salt and cornflour together. Stir in the egg yolks, cream, lemon rind and juice. Whisk the egg white until stiff, then fold into the cheese mixture. Divide between the pastry cases and bake at 180°C/350°F/gas mark 4 for about 25 minutes until risen and golden.

Leave to cool slightly, then remove from the tins and dust lightly with icing sugar. Cut each cheesecake in 6 wedges and serve warm.

PINE CLUSTERS

Toasted pine kernels make these frivolities irresistible!

MAKES ABOUT 20

50g/2oz/¼ cup caster (superfine) sugar
25g/1oz/2 tablespoons unsalted butter
1 teaspoon liquid glucose
1 teaspoon water
100g/4oz/½ cup pine kernels, toasted

Place the sugar in a saucepan over a medium heat and cook to a light caramel colour. Carefully add the butter, glucose and water and cook over a gentle heat until smooth. Stir in the pine kernels and cook for 30 seconds.

Mix well, then drop small spoonfuls of the mixture on to a baking tray lined with baking parchment. Leave to cool until set.

LEMON MERINGUES

MAKES 30

2 egg whites
pinch of salt
100g/4oz/¹/2 cup caster (superfine) sugar

For the filling:
pared rind and juice of 1 lemon
50g/2oz/¹/4 cup unsalted butter
2 egg yolks
100g/4oz/¹/2 cup caster (superfine) sugar
150ml/¹/4 pint/²/3 cup double (heavy) cream

Whisk the egg whites with a pinch of salt in a bowl until stiff, then whisk in the sugar a spoonful at a time until thick and glossy.

Transfer the mixture to a piping bag fitted with a medium star nozzle (tube) and pipe 60 small oblong meringues on to baking trays lined with baking parchment. Bake in a preheated oven at 130°C/250°F/gas mark ¹/2 for 1-1¹/4 hours until the meringues are crisp, dry and easily removed from the paper. Leave to become cold, then store in an airtight container until required.

For the filling, place the lemon rind and juice, butter, egg yolks and sugar in a bowl over a saucepan of simmering water and cook stirring from time to time, for 40-45 minutes until thickened. Pass through a sieve. Leave to go cold.

Whip the cream and fold in the lemon filling. Chill until required. Transfer to a piping bag fitted with a medium star nozzle and pipe a line of lemon cream along the flat side of one of the meringues and sandwich it together with a plain meringue. Repeat until all the meringues are filled.

CARROT CAKE

A fun way to present carrot cake for children and adults alike.

MAKES ABOUT 30

50g/2oz/¹/4 cup skinned hazelnuts, ground
50g/2oz/¹/3 cup ground almonds
3 egg yolks
40g/1¹/2oz/3 tablespoons icing (confectioners')
sugar, sifted
finely grated rind of ¹/4 lemon
15g/¹/2oz/1 tablespoon potato flour
1¹/2 teaspoons baking powder
¹/2 teaspoon ground cinnamon
¹/2 teaspoon ground cloves
100g/4oz/²/3 cup carrot, finely grated
1 tablespoon kirsch
2 egg whites
40g/1¹/2oz/2¹/2 tablespoons caster
(superfine) sugar

For the icing:
175g/6oz/³/4 cup cream cheese
50g/2oz/4¹/2 tablespoons icing (confectioners')
sugar, sifted
50g/2oz/¹/4 cup marzipan (almond paste)
edible orange colouring
angelica or herb such as dill or sweet cicely

Roast the ground nuts in a preheated oven at 180°C/350°F/gas mark 4 for 15-20 minutes until golden.

Whisk the egg yolks, icing sugar and lemon rind until the mixture holds the trail of the whisk. Fold in the dry ingredients, carrots and kirsch until evenly mixed.

Whisk the egg whites until stiff, then whisk in the caster sugar a little at a time until thick. Fold the egg whites into the carrot mixture and transfer to a 20cm/8 inch base-lined cake tin (pan). Bake in a preheated oven at 180°C/350°F/gas mark

4 for about 25 minutes until risen and firm to the touch. Cool on a wire tray.

Beat together the ingredients for the icing and spread over the top of the cake. Cut in about 30 small pieces.

Colour the marzipan with a little orange colouring and shape about 30 miniature carrots. Use a small piece of angelica or herb for the green tops. Place one on each piece of cake.

CHOCOLATE-DIPPED CIGARETTES

Follow the recipe on page 131 for Tuiles, omitting the flaked almonds.

When cooked, roll the biscuits around lightly oiled lengths of thin wooden dowelling or the handles of wooden spoons and leave until crisp.

Dip the ends in melted chocolate, drizzle with fine lines of melted chocolate and leave until set.

The chocolate tuile cornet mixture can also be used to make chocolate cigarettes. Decorate with white chocolate.

PHOTOGRAPH ON PAGE 130

CHOCOLATE TUILE CORNETS

It is best to bake these biscuits in batches of 2 or at most 4 allowing plenty of time to shape them before they go crisp. Whipped cream or pastry cream may be used as alternative fillings.

MAKES ABOUT 20

100g/4oz/9 tablespoons icing (confectioners')
sugar, sifted
100g/4oz/scant 1 cup plain (all-purpose)
flour, sifted
100g/4oz/½ cup unsalted butter, melted
2 egg whites
1 teaspoon vanilla extract
2 teaspoons cocoa powder, sifted
2 teaspoons milk

For the filling:
100g/4oz/4 squares luxury plain
(semisweet) chocolate
120ml/4fl oz/½ cup double (heavy) cream

Sift the icing sugar and flour into a bowl. Quickly stir in the cooled butter, egg whites and vanilla extract to make a smooth paste. Reserve 4 tablespoons of this mixture. Mix the cocoa powder and milk together and add to the bulk of the mixture. Refrigerate for 30 minutes. Place 1½ teaspoon quantities of the chocolate mixture on lightly buttered baking trays or trays lined with baking parchment and spread each one to a round about 7.5cm/3 inch in diameter.

Using a small piping bag fitted with a plain writing nozzle (tube), pipe five lines of the reserved plain mixture across the chocolate mixture and using a skewer, draw lines across the piping in opposite directions to give a feathered effect.

Bake in a preheated oven at 190°C/375°F/gas mark 5 for 4-5 minutes, then remove from the oven and quickly shape each biscuit around a cream horn tin (mould). Leave to cool.

For the filling, place the chocolate and cream in a saucepan and heat gently until the chocolate melts. Remove from the heat and beat well until smooth. Chill until firm, then beat well and using a piping bag fitted with a star nozzle, pipe a little filling into each cornet.

TUILES

Tuiles come in all shapes and forms – they can be left plain or topped with almonds or pistachio nuts and moulded into a wealth of different shapes but one thing they should all have in common is to be feather-light and extremely crisp.

MAKES ABOUT 20

100g/4oz/scant 1 cup plain (all-purpose) flour
100g/4oz/9 tablespoons icing
(confectioners') sugar
100g/4oz/½ cup unsalted butter, melted
2 egg whites
flaked almonds or pistachio nuts to sprinkle
(optional)

Sift the flour and icing sugar into a mixing bowl. Quickly stir in the melted butter and egg whites to make a smooth paste. Refrigerate for 30 minutes.

Line baking trays with baking parchment. Spread 1½ teaspoonful quantities of the mixture into rounds about 7.5cm/3 inches in diameter. Sprinkle with a few flaked nuts, if wished.

Bake in a preheated oven at 190°C/375°F/gas mark 5 for 4-5 minutes until tinged golden at the edges. Carefully remove from the paper and lay over a lightly oiled rolling pin or roll around wooden spoon handles until cold and crisp.

CHOCOLATE-DIPPED CIGARETTES
CHOCOLATE TUILE CORNETS
PLAIN TUILES

BOMBOLINI

MAKES ABOUT 30

15g/1/2oz/1/2 cake fresh (compressed) yeast
50g/2 oz/1/4 cup soft brown sugar
150ml/1/4 pint/2/3 cup milk, warmed
225g/8oz/(scant 2 cups) strong plain (bread)
flour
1/4 teaspoon salt
finely grated rind of 1 small orange
40g/11/2oz/3tbsp unsalted butter
oil for deep frying
apricot jam or small pieces of stem ginger or
almond paste
caster (superfine) sugar
ground cinnamon (optional)

Mix the yeast, sugar and milk with about one quarter of the flour. Leave in a warm place for 10-15 minutes until frothy.

Sift the remaining flour and salt into a bowl and add the orange rind. Rub in the butter, then mix to a soft dough with the yeast liquid. Knead on a lightly floured surface, then place in an oiled bowl, cover and leave to rise in a warm place for about 1 hour or until doubled in size. Break off about 30 small pieces of dough (about 15g/1/2oz each). Flatten each one and place 1/4 teaspoon jam in the centre. Draw the dough around the filling to encase it and re-shape into a ball. Place the dough balls well apart on a greased baking tray (sheet), cover and leave to rise in a warm place for about 15 minutes.

Deep fry the balls in batches – the oil should be about 180°C/350°F – for about 3 minutes or until golden. Drain thoroughly then toss in sugar flavoured with a little cinnamon, if wished.

OPERA SQUARES

A variation on the old-time favourite Gâteau à l'Opéra, for all chocolate lovers.

MAKES ABOUT 50

For the sponge:
3 eggs
75g/3oz/6 tablespoons caster (superfine) sugar
50g/2oz/5 tablespoons plain (all-purpose)
flour, sifted
2 tablespoons dark rum

For the chocolate ganache:
5 tablespoons double (heavy) cream
125g/41/2oz/41/2 squares luxury plain
(semisweet) chocolate
15g/1/2oz/1 tablespoon unsalted butter

For the coffee cream:
150ml/1/4 pint/2/3 cup double (heavy) cream
11/2 teaspoons instant coffee granules
1 teaspoon boiling water
1 tablespoon caster (superfine) sugar

For the chocolate glaze:
75g/3oz/3 squares luxury plain
(semisweet) chocolate
25g/1oz/2 tablespoons unsalted butter

Lightly grease and line the base of a 20cm/8 inch square tin (pan) with greaseproof (wax) paper.

For the sponge, whisk the eggs and sugar with an electric whisk until thick and pale. The whisk should leave a strong trail in the mixture. Fold in the flour and transfer the mixture to the prepared tin. Level the surface and bake in a preheated oven at 220°C/425°F/gas mark 7 for 15-20 minutes until risen and firm to the touch. Cool on a wire tray.

For the chocolate ganache, bring the cream to the boil in a saucepan, then remove from the heat and add the choco-late and butter. Beat well until melted and smooth. Leave to cool to a spreading consistency.

Carefully cut the sponge in three horizontal layers. Line the base of a 18cm/7 inch square tin (pan) with greaseproof (wax) paper and place one layer of sponge in the tin. Sprinkle with 2 teaspoons of the rum.

Spread the chocolate ganache on top and cover with a second layer of sponge. Sprinkle with 2 teaspoons of the rum. Chill until firm.

For the coffee cream, lightly whip the cream. Combine the coffee, water and sugar and fold into the cream. Spread over the chocolate ganache and top with the final layer of sponge. Sprinkle with the remaining rum and chill until firm.

For the chocolate glaze, melt the chocolate and butter together and spread over the top of the assembled cake. Chill for at least 4 hours until set. Cut in squares.

BASIC RECIPES

PROVENÇALE SAUCE

MAKES ABOUT
300ml/½ pint/1¼ cups

50ml/2fl oz/¼ cup olive oil
40g/1½oz/¼ cup onion, finely chopped
2 cloves of garlic, crushed
5 plum tomatoes
250ml/8fl oz/1 cup chicken or vegetable stock
120ml/4fl oz/½ cup dry white wine
1 teaspoon tomato purée (paste)
1 teaspoon freshly chopped oregano
salt and freshly milled pepper

Heat the oil and sweat the onions until translucent. Add the garlic and sweat for a further minute.

Chop four of the tomatoes and add to the onions. Cover and sweat for 5 minutes, then add the stock, white wine, tomato purée, salt and pepper. Simmer for 5 minutes.

Pass the sauce through a fine sieve, then reduce by fast boiling to 300ml/½ pint/1¼ cups.

Blanch, peel, remove the seeds and finely dice the remaining tomato. Add to the sauce with the oregano and season to taste.

ROUILLE

MAKES ABOUT
450ml/¾ pint/2 cups

2 hard-boiled eggs, shelled
1 egg yolk
2 cloves of garlic, crushed
Dijon mustard
300ml/½ pint/1¼ cups olive oil
pinch of saffron threads
salt and freshly milled white pepper

Pass the hard-boiled eggs through a fine sieve, then place in a food processor or liquidiser (blender) with the egg yolk, garlic and mustard to taste. Mix well.

With the food processor working, pour a very thin steady stream of oil into the machine until the mixture is thick and creamy.

Infuse the saffron in a little hot water or white wine and add to the sauce. Season to taste.

APRICOT CHUTNEY

Chutney improves with keeping as the flavours start to develop and mellow. Peaches may be used instead of apricots.

MAKES ABOUT
900g/2lb/4 cups

900g/2lb fresh apricots, halved and stoned (pitted)
50g/2oz/⅓ cup onion, finely chopped
150g/5oz/1 cup sultanas
1 tablespoon ground allspice
½ teaspoon freshly grated ginger
1 clove of garlic, crushed
250ml/8fl oz/1 cup white wine vinegar
salt
300g/10oz/1¼ cups preserving or granulated sugar

Place the apricots, onion, sultanas, allspice, ginger, garlic, vinegar and a sprinkling of salt in a heavy-based saucepan. Bring to the boil, then reduce the heat, cover and simmer for 40 minutes.

Stir in the sugar and cook gently until the sugar is dissolved, then bring to the boil and boil, uncovered, for about 40 minutes, stirring frequently, until the mixture is thickened and the liquid has been absorbed.

Transfer the chutney to a clean hot jar and cover with acid-proof paper. Leave to cool, then cover with a lid. Store in a cool place until required.

FISH MOUSSE

It's a good idea to cook a small amount to test the seasoning.

MAKES A GENEROUS
450g/1lb/2 cups

250g/9oz white fish fillet such as sole or
monkfish, skinned
1 egg white
200ml/7fl oz/scant 1 cup double (heavy) cream
cayenne
salt and freshly milled white pepper

Season the fish fillets with salt and pepper and refrigerate for at least 1 hour. Dry the fish on a kitchen cloth (dish towel), then mince (grind) finely or work in a food processor until smooth. Pass through a fine sieve.

Place the fish in a bowl set over ice and gradually beat in the egg white. Add the cream slowly and continue mixing over the ice until all the cream is incorporated. Season with cayenne, salt and pepper.

CHICKEN FARCE

Use corn-fed or free-range chicken. Grill or fry a small piece of the *farce* to test the seasoning.

MAKES ABOUT
400g/14oz/1¾ cups

1 tablespoon vegetable oil
50g/2oz/⅓ cup onion, finely chopped
1 clove of garlic, crushed
6 coriander (cilantro) stalks, chopped
6 parsley stalks, chopped
300g/10oz/1½ cups boneless chicken meat from
the legs, chopped
1 egg yolk
3 tablespoons double (heavy) cream
salt and freshly milled white pepper

Heat the oil and sweat the onion until translucent. Add the garlic and sweat for a further minute. Add the coriander and parsley stalks. Leave to cool, then add to the chicken.

Mince (grind) the mixture through a medium mincer plate or work in a food processor.

Place the mixture in a bowl set over a bowl of ice and beat in the egg yolk and then the cream. Season generously.

CHICKEN MOUSSE

Use corn-fed or free-range chicken. It's a good idea to cook a tiny amount of the mousse to check the seasoning.

MAKES ABOUT
350g/12oz/1½ cups

1 tablespoon vegetable oil
1 tablespoon chopped onion
200g/7oz chicken breast
1 egg
100ml/3½fl oz/scant ½ cup double
cream, chilled
1 tablespoon freshly chopped herb such as
parsley, chives or coriander (cilantro) (optional)
salt and freshly milled white pepper

Heat the oil and sweat the onion until translucent. Leave to cool. Finely mince (grind) the chicken or work in a food processor with the onion until smooth.

Beat in the egg until the mixture feels stiff. Add the cream slowly, stirring constantly until stiff. Season generously.

DUCK ASPIC

The pig's trotter should release enough strength to set the aspic.

MAKES ABOUT
600ml/1 pint/2½ cups

1 pig's trotter, split
500g/1lb 2oz duck legs, skin removed
100g/4oz/6 tablespoons mixed carrot, leek and celery, finely chopped
2 egg whites
1.5 litres/2½ pints/4½ cups duck or chicken stock
bouquet garni
salt and freshly milled pepper

Place the pig's trotter in cold salted water and bring to the boil. Drain and refresh under cold running water.

Bone out the duck legs, chop the bones and coarsely mince the meat. Combine with the vegetables, egg whites, cold stock and pig's trotter. Add the bouquet garni and season generously. Bring to the boil slowly, stirring occasionally. As soon as a froth forms on top of the stock, stop stirring and simmer very gently for 1 hour.

Season to taste and pass through fine muslin (cheesecloth). Leave to cool, then cover and refrigerate until set.

PESTO

MAKES ABOUT
500ml/18fl oz/2¼ cups

100g/4oz/2 cups basil
50g/2oz/1 cup parsley sprigs
40g/1½oz/¼ cup pine kernels
20g/¾oz/⅓ cup shelled walnuts
20g/¾oz/¼ cup pistachio nuts, skinned
2 cloves of garlic, crushed
1½ teaspoons sea salt
300ml/½ pint/1¼ cups olive oil
freshly milled pepper

Roughly chop the herbs in a food processor. Add all the remaining ingredients and work until the mixture forms a fairly smooth sauce.

SAUCE VIERGE

MAKES ABOUT
450ml/¾ pint/2 cups

120ml/4fl oz/½ cup extra virgin olive oil
40ml/1½fl oz/2⅔ tablespoons balsamic or sherry vinegar
1 teaspoon caster (superfine) sugar
400g/14oz/2½ cups plum tomatoes, blanched, skinned, seeds removed and diced
2 tablespoons finely chopped shallot
2 tablespoons freshly chopped parsley
salt and freshly milled pepper

Whisk together the oil, vinegar and seasonings, then stir in the tomatoes, shallots and parsley. Adjust the seasoning to taste.

CARROT PURÉE

MAKES ABOUT
225g/8oz/1 cup

500g/1lb 2oz/3½ cups carrots, peeled and sliced
40g/1½oz/3 tablespoons unsalted butter
salt and freshly milled pepper

Steam the carrots until tender, then purée in a liquidiser (blender) or food processor. Pass through a fine sieve.

Place the carrot purée in a saucepan and cook over a moderate heat, stirring frequently until the excess liquid has evaporated. Stir in the butter and season to taste.

AÏOLI

MAKES ABOUT
600ml/1 pint/2½ cups

3 egg yolks
1 teaspoon crushed garlic
1 tablespoon Dijon mustard
juice of ½ lemon
400ml/14fl oz/¾ cups olive oil
salt and freshly milled white pepper

Place the egg yolks, garlic, mustard and lemon juice in a food processor or liquidiser (blender) and mix well.

With the food processor working. slowly add the olive oil in a very thin stream until the mixture becomes thick and creamy. Season to taste.

WHITE WINE SAUCE

MAKES ABOUT
150ml/¼ pint/⅔ cup

1 teaspoon finely chopped shallot
12 peppercorns, crushed
120ml/4fl oz/½ cup dry white wine
250ml/8fl oz/1 cup fish stock
120ml/4fl oz/½ cup vegetable stock
120ml/4fl oz/½ cup double (heavy) cream
cayenne
salt

Place the shallot, peppercorns and wine in a saucepan and reduce by two-thirds by fast boiling.

Add the fish and vegetable stocks and reduce again by two-thirds. Add the cream and reduce by half to make about 150ml/¼ pint/⅔ cup sauce. Pass through a fine sieve. Season to taste with cayenne and salt.

RÉMOULADE SAUCE

MAKES ABOUT
150ml/¼ pint/⅔ cup

120ml/4fl oz/½ cup mayonnaise (see page 137)
1 teaspoon Dijon mustard
1 tablespoon freshly chopped chervil and parsley
1 tablespoon finely chopped capers
1 tablespoon finely chopped gherkins
2 anchovy fillets, finely chopped
salt and freshly milled pepper

Combine all the ingredients together in a bowl. Season to taste.

COCKTAIL SAUCE

MAKES ABOUT
200ml/⅓ pint/1 scant cup

150ml/¼ pint/⅔ cup mayonnaise (see page 137)
25ml/1fl oz/2 tablespoons tomato ketchup
1 tablespoon orange juice
1 tablespoon natural yoghurt
1 teaspoon brandy
½ teaspoon freshly chopped dill (optional)
salt and freshly milled pepper

Combine all the ingredients together in a mixing bowl. Season to taste.

CURRY SAUCE

MAKES ABOUT
350ml/12fl oz/1½ cups

50g/2oz/¼ cup unsalted butter or 4 tablespoons vegetable oil
100g/4oz/¾ cup onion, finely chopped
3 cloves of garlic, crushed
1 small green chilli, seeds removed and diced
15g/½oz/4 teaspoons fresh ginger, finely chopped
1 teaspoon coriander seeds, crushed
25g/1oz/½ cup fresh coriander (cilantro) leaves and stalk, chopped
20g/¾oz/4 teaspoons medium-hot curry powder
1 teaspoon turmeric
100g/4oz/¾ cup mango, diced
100g/4oz/¾ cup dessert apple, diced
50g/2oz/⅓ cup pineapple, diced
50g/2oz/⅓ cup banana, diced
300ml/½ pint/1¼ cups vegetable stock
salt

Heat the butter or oil and sweat the onion, garlic, chilli and ginger until the onion is translucent. Add the coriander seeds, fresh coriander, curry powder and turmeric and cook over a gentle heat, stirring, for 1–2 minutes. Add the fruits and cook slowly until they are soft. Add the stock and bring to the boil. Reduce the heat, cover and simmer for 5 minutes.

Cool, then liquidise (blend) until smooth. Pass through a very fine sieve and season with salt to taste.

MUSTARD SAUCE

MAKES ABOUT
250ml/8fl oz/1 cup

1 egg yolk
5 tablespoons sugar syrup (see page 137)
25g/1oz/2 tablespoons Dijon mustard
150ml/¼ pint/⅔ cup vegetable oil
15g/½oz/¼ cup freshly chopped dill
salt and freshly milled white pepper

Whisk the egg yolk, sugar syrup and mustard together in a small bowl. Place over a saucepan of simmering water and cook, stirring, until thickened. Remove from the heat and leave to cool.

Whisk in the oil a few drops at a time until the sauce is very thick. Stir in the dill and season to taste.

GREEN HERB SAUCE

MAKES ABOUT
300ml/½ pint/1¼ cups

50g/2oz/1 cup spinach leaves
200ml/7fl oz/scant 1 cup mayonnaise
(see recipe this page)
2 tablespoons freshly chopped tarragon
salt and freshly milled pepper

Blanch the spinach leaves, then refresh in iced water. Drain and squeeze out excess liquid. Work the spinach to a fine purée in a food processor.

Mix the spinach with the mayonnaise and pass through a fine sieve or muslin (cheesecloth). Stir in the tarragon and season to taste.

BÉCHAMEL SAUCE

MAKES ABOUT
450ml/16fl oz/2 cups

20g/¾oz/1½ tablespoons unsalted butter
25g/1oz/3 tablespoons plain (all-purpose) flour
600ml/1 pint/2½ cups milk
1 small onion spiked with 2 cloves and 1 bay leaf
salt and freshly milled pepper

Melt the butter in a saucepan, add the flour and work together to make a roux. Cook without colouring for about 5 minutes over a gentle heat, then leave to cool.

Bring the milk just to the boil with the prepared onion. Add the milk to the roux slowly, stirring constantly. Cook slowly over a very gentle heat for about 20 minutes. Pass through a fine sieve and season to taste.

MAYONNAISE

To make saffron mayonnaise, infuse a generous pinch of saffron strands in hot water or, dry white wine and add to the prepared mayonnaise as below.

MAKES ABOUT
600ml/1 pint/2½ cups

2 egg yolks
25ml/1fl oz/2 tablespoons white wine vinegar
2 teaspoons Dijon mustard
Worcestershire sauce
500ml/18fl oz/2¼ cups vegetable oil
salt and freshly milled pepper

Combine the egg yolks, vinegar and mustard with a dash of Worcestershire sauce and salt and pepper in a food processor and mix well. Add the oil whilst the machine is working until it has all been incorporated and the mayonnaise is thick. Season to taste.

GARLIC BUTTER

MAKES ABOUT
225g/8oz/1 cup

4 cloves of garlic, peeled
225g/8oz/1 cup unsalted butter, softened
salt and freshly milled white pepper

Blanch the garlic cloves in boiling water. Drain and crush finely.

Add to the butter and beat well until evenly combined. Season to taste.

PASTRY CREAM

MAKES
300ml/½ pint/1¼ cups

300ml/½ pint/1¼ cups milk
1 vanilla pod, split
2 egg yolks
40g/1½oz/2½ tablespoons caster (superfine) sugar
40g/1½oz/¼ cup plain (all-purpose) flour, sifted

Bring the milk to the boil over a gentle heat with the split vanilla pod.

Whisk the egg yolks and sugar together until creamy. Add the flour and mix to a smooth paste. Pour on half of the boiled milk and mix well. Return the mixture to the remaining milk, stirring constantly and cook for 1 minute. Pass through a fine sieve.

SUGAR SYRUP

MAKES ABOUT
600ml/1 pint/2½ cups

250g/9oz/1 cup plus 2 tablespoons caster (superfine) sugar
500ml/18fl oz/2¼ cups water
25ml/1fl oz/2 tablespoons lemon juice

Dissolve the sugar in the water over a gentle heat. Add the lemon juice and bring to the boil.

Leave to cool, then strain through a fine sieve.

CHOUX PASTE

MAKES ABOUT
300g/10oz

120ml/4fl oz/½ cup milk or water
50g/2oz/¼ cup unsalted butter
65g/2½oz/7 tablespoons plain (all-purpose)
flour, sifted
pinch of salt
2 eggs, beaten

Place the milk or water and butter in a saucepan and heat gently until the butter is melted, then bring to the boil. Add the flour and beat constantly until the mixture forms a ball of paste which comes away from the side of the saucepan easily. Cook for 30 seconds, stirring constantly.

Allow to cool slightly, then beat in the egg a little at a time until the mixture is thick and glossy.

SWEET PASTRY

MAKES ABOUT
350g/12oz

100g/4oz/½ cup unsalted butter
50g/2oz/¼ cup caster (superfine) sugar
2 tablespoons beaten egg
175g/6oz/1⅓ cups plain (all-purpose)
flour, sifted
pinch of salt

Cream the butter and sugar together until pale.

Beat in the egg then slowly add the flour with a pinch of salt and mix to a smooth paste.

Cover and leave to rest in the refrigerator for at least 1 hour.

NUT PASTRY

MAKES ABOUT
350g/12oz

75g/3oz/6 tablespoons unsalted butter
100g/4oz/scant 1 cup plain (all-purpose) flour
75g/3oz/6 tablespoons assorted nuts such as
walnuts and skinned hazelnuts, finely grated
or ground
¼ teaspoon almond extract
1 tablespoon beaten egg

Combine all the ingredients in a food processor and work to form a smooth paste.

Alternatively, rub the butter into the flour, then add the nuts and sugar. Stir in the almond extract and beaten egg and work to a smooth paste.

SHORTCRUST PASTRY

MAKES ABOUT
300g/10oz

50g/1¾oz/¼ cup unsalted butter, cut in
small dice
50g/1¾oz/¼ cup lard or other white fat, cut in
small dice
200g/7oz/1⅔ cups plain (all-purpose) flour,
sifted
pinch of salt
7 teaspoons cold water

Rub the butter and lard into the flour with a pinch of salt until the mixture resembles fine crumbs.

Add the water and quickly mix to a smooth paste. Cover and leave to rest in the refrigerator for about 20 minutes.

NOTE For this recipe the weight of the combined fats should be exactly half the weight of the flours; therefore the imperial quantities differ from the standard conversion used throughout this book.

MENU SUGGESTIONS

CANAPÉS BEFORE LUNCH

Canapés before lunch create the ambience and atmosphere of the lunch itself.

The guidelines are fairly obvious. It's best to prepare a selection of very light, healthy and interesting canapés which are not too complex in taste nor too sophisticated in preparation. As a rule of thumb, make four or five variations and prepare two or three of each kind for each guest. One or two hot ones are sufficient.

As your guests arrive, serve half the cold canapés or place them strategically around the room. When everybody has arrived, serve the hot canapes at once and then the remaining cold ones but do stop serving at least 15 minutes before sitting down to lunch – the idea being to excite but not dull the appetite.

SUGGESTION 1

Salmon Carpaccio
Cucumber Teasers
Gourmet Delight
Spiced Nuts
Pesto Moons

SUGGESTION 2

Dip and Dive
(with only one dip so it will not be too confusing)
Grissini Francesca
Pastrami and Pickles
Italian Crostini
Puffs

WINTER CANAPÉS IN PLACE OF LUNCH OR DINNER

Something quite substantial is obviously needed in this instance.

Seasonal influences must be taken into consideration when choosing the canapés but it isn't always necessary to serve a great variety of them. Sometimes it's nice just to serve one or two varieties at the same time and offer them over quite a lengthy period of time, say 20 minutes.

For the first 20 minutes or so when you are welcoming your guests and waiting for everyone to arrive, offer just one warm canapé.

SUGGESTION 1

Game and Chestnut Chipolatas
(which are unusual and fairly spicy)
Japanese Mushroom Cups
Rillette on Garlic Croûtes
Fantasy of Smoked Salmon

After all these, serve the main dishes of the reception.

New York Crab Cakes
Lentil Burgers
Trendy Yorkshire Puddings

Followed with a cheese savoury such as:

Reblochon and Radish Croûtes

To finish, offer:

Lemon Feuilletés
Tuiles

SUGGESTION 2

Allow about 3 pieces of each canapé per person.

Langoustines in their Pyjamas with Mango Sauce
Mushroom or Radish Whirls
Belgian Endive (Chicory) Spikes
Salmon Tartare on Rye
Peppered Mussels
Brioche Soufflés
Ham and Asparagus Kisses
Warm Goat's Cheese in a Seed Crust

Scones with Exotic Fruits
Toffee Tartlets

SUMMERTIME

Sunny days and blue skies with canapés and frivolities can be an ideal combination. This is what dreams are made of.

Do try to pick dishes which can be prepared quite well in advance so you can enjoy the party, and the sun, just as much as your guests!

SUGGESTION 1

Plantain Crisps
Pastrami and Pickles
Crab Chequerboard
Onion Wedges
Evesham Clusters
Tomato and Beansprout Croûtes
Fresh Fig, Cheese and Strawberry Biscuits
Filo Tulips with Greek Yoghurt and Yellow Fruits
Lemon Meringues

SUGGESTION 2

Paillettes
Kiwi Bites
Quails' Egg Koftas
Spicy Vine Leaves
Riviera Tartlets
Onions and Nuts
Crisp Courgéttes (Zucchini) with Pesto
Scallop Croûtes with Sauce Vierge
Chicken Skewers with Bacon

Caramelised Apples with Blue Cheese
Marinated Strawberries
Chocolate Tuile Cornets

UNFORGETTABLE MENUS

We all know that there are very special occasions in our lives, be they of a personal nature, business or family celebrations, or simply a time to spoil oneself. It is often the surprise party for just one such occasion that you remember for years to come.

Here are two suggestions for unforgettable menus to serve on these special occasions.

As the dishes are expensive and of the highest quality you do not need to prepare many of them. Two pieces per person is enough.

SUGGESTION 1

Belgian Oysters
Black Sea Blinis
Goose Liver Pâté Eclairs
Quails Egg Tartlets with Truffle Butter
Seabass Flutes
Celery Barquettes
Loganberry Palmiers
Black and White Chocolate Pralines

SUGGESTION 2

Moscovite Potatoes
Lobster with Asparagus
Cocktail Tomatoes
Brie Tartlets
Salmon in a Pastry Trellis
Marinated Chicken Alanya
Fritto Misto in Chilli Batter
Angels on Horseback

Opera Squares
Strawberry Tartlets
Rendez-vous of Fruits with Fruit Coulis

ORIENTAL TITBITS

What can be more fascinating than the exotic tastes and fragrances of the Far East?

You may think that oriental food is too difficult to produce, but some is not as complex as you may imagine and many of the ingredients are now readily available in oriental stores and some supermarkets.

You will be well rewarded by your efforts; giving utter satisfaction to your taste buds and sheer delight to the eye. The presentation of these most attractive foods can be spectacular.

Serve at least 4 or 5 variations at the same time for maximum impact.

Prawn Toasts
Thai Curry Bites
Scampi Tails in Red Curry Sauce
Pork Balls in Golden Threads
Satay
Prawn (Shrimp) and Bamboo Shoot Wonton
Pigeon Tikka
Vegetable Samosas

Miniature Syrup Tarts
Minted Melon Balls

INDEX

Italic numbers refer to recipe photographs.